STRESS FREE LIVING

STRESS FREE LIVING

DR. TREVOR POWELL

DK PUBLISHING, INC.

A DORLING KINDERSLEY BOOK
www.dk.com

*This book is dedicated to my parents
Ron and Fay Powell!*

Produced for DK Publishing Inc., by
PAGE*One*, Cairn House, Elgiva Lane, Chesham,
Buckinghamshire HP5 2JD

PROJECT DIRECTORS Helen Parker, Bob Gordon

SENIOR EDITOR Charlotte Davies
SENIOR MANAGING EDITOR Mary-Clare Jerram
MANAGING ART EDITOR Amanda Lunn
PRODUCTION CONTROLLER Michelle Thomas
US EDITOR Laaren Brown

First paperback edition, 2000
First American edition, 1997
2 4 6 8 10 9 7 5 3 1

Published in the United States by DK Publishing, Inc.
95 Madison Avenue, New York, New York 10016
Visit us on the World Wide Web at
http://www.dk.com

Library of Congress Cataloging-in-Publication Data
Powell, Trevor J. [1953 -]
Stress free living / by Trevor Powell
DK Living Series
p.   cm
Includes Hardcover index.
ISBN 0–7894–5119–0 Paperback
ISBN 0–7894–1475–9 Hardcover
1. Stress management. 2. Stress (Psychology)
3. Adjustment (Psychology) I. Title.
RA785.P697   1996
155.9′ 042--dc20   96-33598
                                        CIP

Color reproduction by Colourpath, England
Printed and bound in Singapore by Star Standard
Industries (Pte.) Ltd.

CONTENTS

PART ONE

SIGNS OF STRESS

WHAT IS STRESS?

We all experience stress, which can affect us in many different ways.
A certain level of stress is beneficial and stimulates us to perform well,
but too much stress can impair performance.

Stress is a positive force that enables you to survive. When you are waiting to cross a busy road you need to be temporarily stressed. Because you are alert, vigilant, and aware of danger, you are more likely to cross safely. Like an electric current, stress increases arousal, gives you energy, and improves your performance. However, if the current is turned up too high, stress can produce unpleasant effects and cause your performance to deteriorate. Conversely, too little stress can cause you to feel listless and unstimulated, and you are likely to perform slowly and inefficiently. A definition of too much stress might be when you see your environment as taxing or exceeding your ability to cope, endangering your well-being. Stress has three basic components:

LIVING WITH STRESS
Stress is a positive, motivating force that affects you to some degree throughout your life (*above*), whether you are a child at school, a university student, a parent, company director, unemployed worker, or retired. Only when demands outweigh your ability to cope does stress start to have negative effects.

HOW STRESS AFFECTS YOUR PERFORMANCE
The Yorkes-Dodson Law states that a certain level of stimulation improves performance. This illustration (*right*) shows how you might perform if you were asked to separate colored counters into different bottles under the following conditions:
A – with no time limit;
B – with financial reward related to speed and accuracy;
C – with the punishment of an electric shock if you perform slowly or inaccurately.

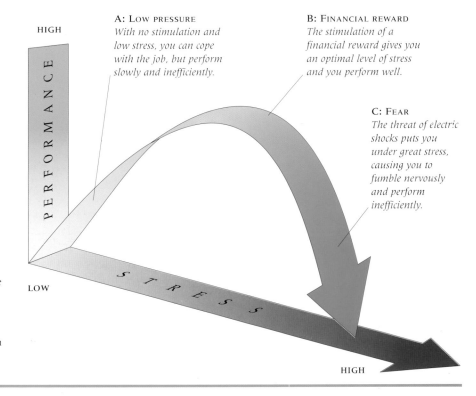

A: LOW PRESSURE
With no stimulation and low stress, you can cope with the job, but perform slowly and inefficiently.

B: FINANCIAL REWARD
The stimulation of a financial reward gives you an optimal level of stress and you perform well.

C: FEAR
The threat of electric shocks puts you under great stress, causing you to fumble nervously and perform inefficiently.

HIGH

PERFORMANCE

LOW

STRESS

HIGH

■ SOURCES These are everyday demands or major changes in your life. Part Two of this book reveals individual sources of stress.
■ LIFE SKILLS These are the resources you have for coping with stressful events. Important life skills are examined in Part Three.
■ SIGNS OR SYMPTOMS These are physical and emotional symptoms that indicate that the demands outweigh your resources to cope. A range of symptoms is covered in Part One.

THE STRESS-RESISTANT PERSONALITY

Recent studies have found that people with high levels of stress but low levels of illness share three characteristics, which are sometimes referred to as the three "C"s. Stress-resistant personalities have:
■ CONTROL – a sense of purpose and direction in their life.
■ COMMITMENT – to work, hobbies, social life, or family.
■ CHALLENGE – seeing changes in life as normal and positive rather than as a threat. However, not everyone is born with these characteristics, and many people have to relearn specific life skills in areas such as assertiveness or rational thinking to equip them better to cope with the demands of everyday life.

COPING WITH STRESS
The way you cope with stress often depends on rigid, deep-seated beliefs, based on experience. You may feel angry in a traffic jam, because you believe that the traffic "should" move faster. To manage stress, you often need to reassess the way you think and learn coping strategies.

EFFECTS OF STRESS

BODY
Increased heart rate
High blood pressure
Difficulty in breathing
Difficulty in swallowing
Feelings of nausea
Hyperventilation
Tense, contracted muscles
Backache
Immune system less efficient
Hot and cold flashes
Blushing
Sweating
Skin dryness
Rashes
Numbness
Tingling sensations
Increased blood sugar levels
Dilation of pupils, dry mouth
Frequent urination

BEHAVIOR
Difficulty in sleeping
Early awakening
Emotional outbursts
Aggression
Overeating or loss of appetite
Excessive drinking
Excessive smoking/drug taking
Accident proneness/trembling
Avoidance of particular situations
Inactivity

THOUGHTS
Difficulty in concentrating
Difficulty in making decisions
Frequent forgetfulness
Increased sensitivity to criticism
Negative self-critical thoughts
Distorted ideas
More rigid attitudes

EMOTIONS
Anxiety (nervousness, tension, phobias, panics)
Depression (sadness, lowered self-esteem, apathy, fatigue)
Guilt and shame
Moodiness
Loneliness
Jealousy

HEALTH
Coronary heart disease/strokes
Stomach ulcers; nausea; irritable bowel syndrome
Migraine; headaches
Asthma; hay fever
Skin rashes
Irregular menstruation
Diarrhea
Cancer

STRESS AND YOUR BODY

When you find yourself in a potentially threatening situation, such as just before an exam or waiting to go into the hospital for an operation, a complex series of biochemical and physiological events occurs in your body to prepare you for action. Often called the "fight or flight" response, this reaction can be traced back to our evolutionary past where, for our early ancestors, survival depended on being able to outrun or overpower dangerous predators. We still use the fight or flight response today, although it is now triggered by more subtle situations and we are often not even conscious of them.

When the source of threat is removed or resolved, the fight or flight response diminishes, and your body returns to a stable state. This process is known as homeostasis. Imagine that you are sitting at home late at night when you hear a noise outside the window. You may think that it is a burglar trying to break in. Your body immediately goes into a state of high arousal as you prepare for action. Your heart beats faster, your mouth gets dry, and your muscles tense. However, if you discover it is your neighbor, your perception of the situation alters. You do not feel in danger, and your body functions return to normal. The type and level of physiological arousal you are likely to have in a threatening situation are largely determined by your thoughts and interpretation of how much danger you are in.

KEEPING FIT
Physical exercise helps boost the immune system and increases the activity of natural killer cells, which destroy foreign bodies, preventing illness and disease.

EFFECTS ON IMMUNE SYSTEM

Prolonged periods of stress, where the body does not return to a homeostatic state, can result in chronic exhaustion and illness. Research has shown that groups of people undergoing stressful life crises, such as bereavement, marital breakdown, or depression, show significant impairment in their immune system.

Under constant stress, the body continues to manufacture increased quantities of stress chemicals, particularly cortisol, which depresses the immune system. Tests on people suffering from high levels of stress have shown a reduction in the activity of the aptly named NK or natural killer cells. These are the cells that circulate in the blood ready to attack foreign bodies and destroy any mutant or cancerous cells. Further research has shown that relaxation training increases NK cell activity, thus strengthening the immune system.

REACTIONS TO PROLONGED STRESS

When you are under stress, you start to notice signs such as some of those listed below. These are triggered by a number of physiological changes as your body prepares for action.

SIGNS OF STRESS

Difficulty swallowing

Aching neck, backache, muscle tension, fatigue, muscle pain

Hyperventilation, panic, chest pains, tingling, palpitations, asthma

High blood pressure

Rapid fatigue

Nausea, indigestion, heartburn, ulcers

Excess sweating, blushing, skin dryness, rashes

Frequent urination, diarrhea

Immune system less efficient

PHYSICAL REACTIONS

Pupils dilate, mouth goes dry – saliva decreases

Neck and shoulder muscles tense – all large skeletal muscles contract for action

Breathing becomes faster and shallower supplying more oxygen for muscles

Heart pumps faster – blood vessels dilate, so blood flows to brain and muscles

Liver releases stored sugar to provide fuel for quick energy

Digestion slows down or ceases as blood is diverted away from the stomach

Blood vessels and capillaries move to skin surface to cool body by perspiration

Muscles at the opening of anus and bladder are relaxed

Cortisol, adrenaline, and noradrenalin are released

A MODEL OF STRESS

Like a set of weighing scales, you are constantly trying to find a balance between the demands imposed upon you by everyday life and your capabilities to cope. If perceived demands outweigh your perception of your capabilities, the scales tip, you are unbalanced, and you begin to experience symptoms of stress. In all areas of life, whether in work, sports, education, or the arts, the best performances occur when we are on that "knife edge," where there is a tension, but also a balance, between demands and capabilities.

SOURCES

Everyone has demands placed on them by everyday life, and as one small thing is piled onto the next, the scales can finally be tipped off balance by a seemingly insignificant "last straw," which may be something as trivial as one too many telephone calls.

Alternatively, demands can increase quite suddenly as a result of significant changes or life events. Research shows a link between the number of significant life events and stress-related ill health.

LIFE SKILLS

On the other side of the scales, counterbalancing these demands are your capabilities or coping skills, which are learned throughout your life. The more you are able to develop and improve your life skills, the more demands you will be able to cope with on the other side of the scales. It also seems that the better your coping skills the more control you have over the demands that come into your life. Those with poor coping skills are constantly being buffeted by uncontrollable, unforeseen demands and are not able to anticipate or regulate oncoming difficulties. None of us can be in complete control of our lives, because fate is likely to occasionally throw unexpected demands at us. However, the ability to regulate significant life events is fundamental to efficient stress management.

LIFE SKILLS

Your ability to cope depends on how well prepared you are to deal with and counterbalance everyday demands, and keep an equilibrium in your life. All of these life skills can be learned and improved upon. The main skills are:

how assertively you behave • how rationally you think • how effectively you organize your life • the quality and quantity of your relationships • how well you look after yourself

SIGNS

When perceived demands outweigh perceived capabilities, the scales tip, there is an imbalance, and you suffer physical and emotional symptoms of stress. The particular area in which symptoms occur is usually determined by your family background and genetic temperament. One unpleasant consequence of these physical symptoms is that they invariably become a secondary stress in themselves. For example, if you have a panic attack as the result of an excess of demands, you may become more worried by a possible second attack than by the initial stresses that caused it. A vicious cycle can develop where primary stresses cause physical symptoms that themselves become added, secondary stresses. These secondary stresses often cause more symptoms than the primary stresses.

YOUR PERCEPTIONS

It is important to remember that any stress you experience is a result of your interpretation of the demands and your capabilities to cope not the demands and capabilities themselves. Your perception of the sources of stress and your ability to cope depend largely on your past experiences. For example, an experienced racing car driver might not feel any stress driving at 125mph (200km/h) but would be very stressed if asked to deliver a lecture to 200 students. An experienced lecturer, on the other hand, might not worry about making a speech but might be terrified by driving at high speed. We all have different experiences, skills, expectations, and abilities to cope differently with different situations. One person's stress is another person's relaxation.

SIGNS

When there is an imbalance between the demands of everyday life and your ability to cope, you are likely to show physical or emotional signs of stress, which may include:

headaches • muscle tension • palpitations • panic attacks • diarrhea • low self-esteem • depression fatigue • anger • phobias eating disorders • drinking smoking • sleep problems obsessive behavior

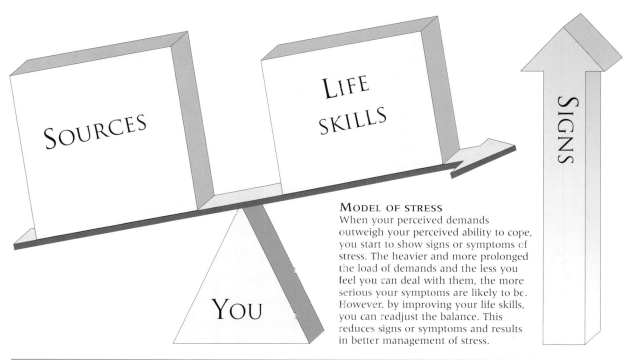

MODEL OF STRESS
When your perceived demands outweigh your perceived ability to cope, you start to show signs or symptoms of stress. The heavier and more prolonged the load of demands and the less you feel you can deal with them, the more serious your symptoms are likely to be. However, by improving your life skills, you can readjust the balance. This reduces signs or symptoms and results in better management of stress.

HOW TO USE THIS BOOK

Free Yourself from Harmful Stress is divided into three sections, each of which is introduced by an in-depth questionnaire. Searching questions and commonsense interpretations help you to understand if stress is a problem for you, and if so, what causes it, how you react, and which areas you need to work on. Each section is color-coded in a different tint for easy reference.

Parts One and Two help you to recognize and identify the signs and likely sources of stress and provide concise solutions to help you manage in the short term. Each subject is fully cross-referenced to the essential life skills covered in Part Three. This final section offers practical, long-term programs and strategies for coping with everyday demands as well as significant life events.

QUESTIONNAIRES

Each section of the book is introduced by a double-page questionnaire to help you identify which of the following pages can offer you most help. Mini-questionnaires throughout the book enable you to assess specific areas, which you need to work on.

SCORING

Helpful scores alert you to how stressed you are overall and refer you the following section to find useful solutions that are most relevant to you personally.

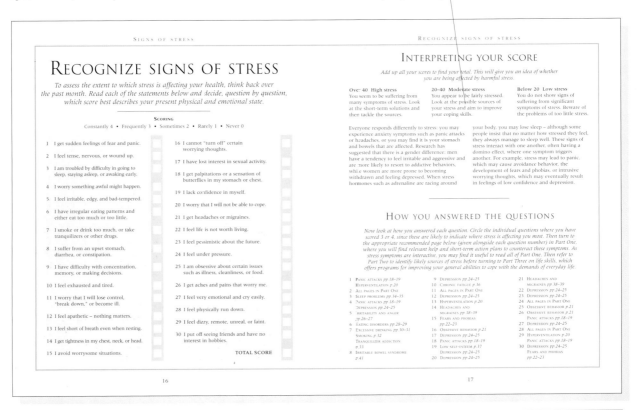

RECOGNIZE SIGNS OF STRESS

To assess the extent to which stress is affecting your health, think back over the past month. Read each of the statements below and decide, question by question, which score best describes your present physical and emotional state.

SCORING

Constantly 4 • Frequently 3 • Sometimes 2 • Rarely 1 • Never 0

1   I get sudden feelings of fear and panic.

2   I feel tense, nervous, or wound up.

3   I am troubled by difficulty in going to sleep, staying asleep, or awaking early.

4   I worry something awful might happen.

5   I feel irritable, edgy, and bad-tempered.

6   I have irregular eating patterns and either eat too much or too little.

7   I smoke or drink too much, or take tranquilizers or other drugs.

8   I suffer from an upset stomach, diarrhea, or constipation.

9   I have difficulty with concentration, memory, or making decisions.

10 I feel exhausted and tired.

11 I worry that I will lose control, "break down," or become ill.

12 I feel apathetic – nothing matters.

13 I feel short of breath even when resting.

14 I get tightness in my chest, neck, or head.

15 I avoid worrysome situations.

16 I cannot "turn off" certain worrying thoughts.

17 I have lost interest in sexual activity.

18 I get palpitations or a sensation of butterflies in my stomach or chest.

19 I lack confidence in myself.

20 I worry that I will not be able to cope.

21 I get headaches or migraines.

22 I feel life is not worth living.

23 I feel pessimistic about the future.

24 I feel under pressure.

25 I am obsessive about certain issues such as illness, cleanliness, or food.

26 I get aches and pains that worry me.

27 I feel very emotional and cry easily.

28 I feel physically run down.

29 I feel dizzy, remote, unreal, or faint.

30 I put off seeing friends and have no interest in hobbies.

TOTAL SCORE

INTERPRETING YOUR SCORE

Add up all your scores to find your total. This will give you an idea of whether you are being affected by harmful stress.

Over 40 High stress
You seem to be suffering from many symptoms of stress. Look at the short-term solutions and then tackle the sources.

20–40 Moderate stress
You appear to be fairly stressed. Look at the possible sources of your stress and aim to improve your coping skills.

Below 20 Low stress
You do not show signs of suffering from significant symptoms of stress. Beware of the problems of too little stress.

Everyone responds differently to stress: you may experience anxiety symptoms such as panic attacks or headaches, or you may find it is your stomach and bowels that are affected. Research has suggested that there is a gender difference: men have a tendency to feel irritable and aggressive and are more likely to resort to addictive behaviors, while women are more prone to becoming withdrawn and feeling depressed. When stress hormones such as adrenaline are racing around your body, you may lose sleep – although some people insist that no matter how stressed they feel, they always manage to sleep well. These signs of stress interact with one another, often having a domino effect, where one symptom triggers another. For example, stress may lead to panic, which may cause avoidance behavior, the development of fears and phobias, or intrusive worrying thoughts, which may eventually result in feelings of low confidence and depression.

HOW YOU ANSWERED THE QUESTIONS

Now look at how you answered each question. Circle the individual questions where you have scored 3 or 4, since these are likely to indicate where stress is affecting you most. Then turn to the appropriate recommended page below (given alongside each question number) in Part One, where you will find relevant help and short-term action plans to counteract these symptoms. As stress symptoms are interactive, you may find it useful to read all of Part One. Then refer to Part Two to identify likely sources of stress before turning to Part Three on life skills, which offers programs for improving your general abilities to cope with the demands of everyday life.

1 PANIC ATTACKS *pp 18–19*
   HYPERVENTILATION *p 20*

2 ALL PAGES IN PART ONE

3 SLEEP PROBLEMS *pp 34–35*

4 PANIC ATTACKS *pp 18–19*
   DEPRESSION *pp 24–25*

5 IRRITABILITY AND ANGER *pp 26–27*

6 EATING DISORDERS *pp 30–31*
   SMOKING *p 32*
   TRANQUILIZER ADDICTION *p 33*

7 IRRITABLE BOWEL SYNDROME *p 41*

9 CHRONIC FATIGUE *p 36*

10 ALL PAGES IN PART ONE

11 DEPRESSION *pp 24–25*

12 HYPERVENTILATION *p 20*

13 HEADACHES AND MIGRAINES *pp 38–39*

14 FEARS AND PHOBIAS *pp 22–23*

15 OBSESSIVE BEHAVIOR *p 21*

16 OBSESSIVE BEHAVIOR *p 21*

17 DEPRESSION *pp 24–25*

18 PANIC ATTACKS *pp 18–19*

19 LOW SELF-ESTEEM *p 37*
    DEPRESSION *pp 24–25*

20 DEPRESSION *pp 24–25*

21 HEADACHES AND MIGRAINES *pp 38–39*

22 DEPRESSION *pp 24–25*

23 DEPRESSION *pp 24–25*

24 ALL PAGES IN PART ONE

25 OBSESSIVE BEHAVIOR *p 21*

26 OBSESSIVE BEHAVIOR *p 21*
    PANIC ATTACKS *pp 18–19*

27 DEPRESSION *pp 24–25*

28 HYPERVENTILATION *p 20*

29 PANIC ATTACKS *pp 18–19*

30 DEPRESSION *pp 24–25*
    FEARS AND PHOBIAS *pp 22–23*

16

17

SIGNS OF STRESS
Part One looks at the physical and emotional signs that indicate your level of stress. Work through this section before turning to Part Two.

SHORT-TERM SOLUTIONS
Useful tips in Parts One and Two offer short-term solutions for managing stress.

CROSS REFERENCES
Essential life skills relevant to each symptom are cross-referenced in Parts One and Two.

SOURCES OF STRESS
Part Two looks at the demands of everyday life and significant life events that may be causing you to feel stressed. Identify your sources of stress, then turn to Part Three.

SMALL BOXES
Boxes surrounded by a colored rule contain questions, facts, lists, and information to help you understand the content of the pages.

LIFE SKILLS
Part Three offers practical, self-help programs and specific coping strategies for improving your life skills and preparing yourself for the demands of everyday life.

LONG-TERM PROGRAMS
In Part Three, practical programs help you identify areas of weakness and show you how to improve and strengthen life skills in the long term.

SIGNS *of* STRESS

RECOGNIZE SIGNS OF STRESS

To assess the extent to which stress is affecting your health, think back over the past month. Read each of the statements below and decide, question by question, which score best describes your present physical and emotional state.

SCORING
Constantly 4 • Frequently 3 • Sometimes 2 • Rarely 1 • Never 0

1 I get sudden feelings of fear and panic.

2 I feel tense, nervous, or wound up.

3 I am troubled by difficulty in going to sleep, staying asleep, or awaking early.

4 I worry something awful might happen.

5 I feel irritable, edgy, and bad-tempered.

6 I have irregular eating patterns and either eat too much or too little.

7 I smoke or drink too much, or take tranquilizers or other drugs.

8 I suffer from an upset stomach, diarrhea, or constipation.

9 I have difficulty with concentration, memory, or making decisions.

10 I feel exhausted and tired.

11 I worry that I will lose control, "break down," or become ill.

12 I feel apathetic – nothing matters.

13 I feel short of breath even when resting.

14 I get tightness in my chest, neck, or head.

15 I avoid worrisome situations.

16 I cannot "turn off" certain worrying thoughts.

17 I have lost interest in sexual activity.

18 I get palpitations or a sensation of butterflies in my stomach or chest.

19 I lack confidence in myself.

20 I worry that I will not be able to cope.

21 I get headaches or migraines.

22 I feel life is not worth living.

23 I feel pessimistic about the future.

24 I feel under pressure.

25 I am obsessive about certain issues such as illness, cleanliness, or food.

26 I get aches and pains that worry me.

27 I feel very emotional and cry easily.

28 I feel physically run down.

29 I feel dizzy, remote, unreal, or faint.

30 I put off seeing friends and have no interest in hobbies.

TOTAL SCORE

INTERPRETING YOUR SCORE

Add up all your scores to find your total. This will give you an idea of whether you are being affected by harmful stress.

Over 40 High stress
You seem to be suffering from many symptoms of stress. Look at the short-term solutions and then tackle the sources.

20–40 Moderate stress
You appear to be fairly stressed. Look at the possible sources of your stress and aim to improve your coping skills.

Below 20 Low stress
You do not show signs of suffering from significant symptoms of stress. Beware of the problems of too little stress.

Everyone responds differently to stress: you may experience anxiety symptoms such as panic attacks or headaches, or you may find it is your stomach and bowels that are affected. Research has suggested that there is a gender difference: men have a tendency to feel irritable and aggressive and are more likely to resort to addictive behaviors, while women are more prone to becoming withdrawn and feeling depressed. When stress hormones such as adrenaline are racing around your body, you may lose sleep – although some people insist that no matter how stressed they feel, they always manage to sleep well. These signs of stress interact with one another, often having a domino effect, where one symptom triggers another. For example, stress may lead to panic, which may cause avoidance behavior, the development of fears and phobias, or intrusive worrying thoughts, which may eventually result in feelings of low confidence and depression.

HOW YOU ANSWERED THE QUESTIONS

Now look at how you answered each question. Circle the individual questions where you have scored 3 or 4, since these are likely to indicate where stress is affecting you most. Then turn to the appropriate recommended page below (given alongside each question number) in Part One, where you will find relevant help and short-term action plans to counteract these symptoms. As stress symptoms are interactive, you may find it useful to read all of Part One. Then refer to Part Two to identify likely sources of stress before turning to Part Three on life skills, which offers programs for improving your general abilities to cope with the demands of everyday life.

1 PANIC ATTACKS *pp.18–19*
   HYPERVENTILATION *p.20*
2 ALL PAGES IN PART ONE
3 SLEEP PROBLEMS *pp.34–35*
4 PANIC ATTACKS *pp.18–19*
   DEPRESSION *pp.24–25*
5 IRRITABILITY AND ANGER *pp.26–27*
6 EATING DISORDERS *pp.28–29*
7 EXCESSIVE DRINKING *pp.30–31*
   SMOKING *p.32*
   TRANQUILIZER ADDICTION *p.33*
8 IRRITABLE BOWEL SYNDROME *p.41*

9 DEPRESSION *pp.24–25*
10 CHRONIC FATIGUE *p.36*
11 ALL PAGES IN PART ONE
12 DEPRESSION *pp.24–25*
13 HYPERVENTILATION *p.20*
14 HEADACHES AND MIGRAINES *pp.38–39*
15 FEARS AND PHOBIAS *pp.22–23*
16 OBSESSIVE BEHAVIOR *p.21*
17 DEPRESSION *pp.24–25*
18 PANIC ATTACKS *pp.18–19*
19 LOW SELF-ESTEEM *p.37*
   DEPRESSION *pp.24–25*
20 DEPRESSION *pp.24–25*

21 HEADACHES AND MIGRAINES *pp.38–39*
22 DEPRESSION *pp.24–25*
23 DEPRESSION *pp.24–25*
24 ALL PAGES IN PART ONE
25 OBSESSIVE BEHAVIOR *p.21*
26 OBSESSIVE BEHAVIOR *p.21*
   PANIC ATTACKS *pp.18–19*
27 DEPRESSION *pp.24–25*
28 ALL PAGES IN PART ONE
29 HYPERVENTILATION *p.20*
   PANIC ATTACKS *pp.18–19*
30 DEPRESSION *pp.24–25*
   FEARS AND PHOBIAS *pp.22–23*

PANIC ATTACKS

*"Suddenly, for no obvious reason, my heart starts pounding.
I feel dizzy, I'm sweating and shaking, I'm terrified
that I'm going to faint or completely lose control."*

Feelings of panic are normal and harmless.

Panic attacks are among the most frightening symptoms of stress and are experienced by approximately one in ten adults. If you have never had a panic attack, it is difficult to understand what the sufferer goes through. Imagine that you are sitting on a train on your way to visit a friend, when you notice a masked man enter your carriage waving a machine gun. Quite naturally you panic – your heart begins to race, you break out in a sweat, shake, and you try to work out how you can escape. Now imagine experiencing the same feelings of terror, on the same train journey, but for no apparent reason. There is nothing there – just other travelers quietly talking and reading their newspapers. As you try desperately to make sense of what is happening, your mind leaps to wild conclusions and you probably think, "I'm going crazy… I'm having a heart attack… I'm going to make a fool of myself… I'm losing control… I'm going to die."

PANIC IS A NORMAL RESPONSE TO FEAR

Everybody has experienced these frightening symptoms, as the body's so-called "fight or flight" response. Imagine the physical feelings associated with a near miss in a car accident. Your body automatically goes into a state of high arousal as it prepares to cope with danger. This immediate, physical response can be traced back thousands of years to our prehistoric ancestors who had to fight or run away from wild animals in order to survive. In the face of danger, adrenaline is released making the heart pump faster to increase the blood supply to the muscles in the limbs, breathing speeds up to take in more oxygen, and sweating cools the body. This same reflex reaction lies at the heart of panic attacks. The difference is that, although it has exactly the same physical effects, it now occurs in situations where there is no obvious danger. We must constantly remind ourselves that a panic attack, which might occur in a supermarket, or in a meeting at work, has its roots in this life-saving response. A panic attack will not harm you. You will not faint, go crazy, or have a heart attack.

WHAT MAKES ME PANIC?

A panic attack may appear to come "out of the blue," but you will usually find that the major trigger is an overload of stresses, worries, and life events that reverberates between your conscious and unconscious mind. This build-up of internal stresses, combined with being in a situation where you may feel slightly trapped or threatened, is often enough to cause unpleasant physical sensations. Your natural reaction is firstly to

"I think I'm having a heart attack – I'm going to die."

misinterpret these symptoms, thinking that something is seriously wrong or is about to happen to you, such as you are having a heart attack, dying, or going crazy. A second natural reaction is to want to escape or run away.

DOWNWARD SPIRAL OF PANIC

The three factors – physical symptoms, worrying thoughts, and avoidance behavior – feed off and perpetuate each other to create a downward spiral of panic. Once you have had one panic attack you are always looking for signs of another – you become over-vigilant, sensitized to minor bodily symptoms that you would have previously ignored. If you start to misinterpret what is happening, you become more anxious, you have irrational thoughts, and you start to panic. Remember that, although they are unpleasant and frightening, panic attacks are harmless. If you start to avoid certain situations for fear of having an attack, you risk progressively losing your mobility. In your mind, the fear of an attack grows, whereas if you can understand and confront your fear, you will realize that you are able to cope with and conquer it (see pp.22–23).

Don't avoid. Stay in the situation and wait for your anxiety to fade away.

WHEN DO PANIC ATTACKS OCCUR?

You are most likely to suffer a panic attack when you are feeling tired or run down, and consequently less well equipped to cope with the stresses of daily life. If you find that stress tends to affect your breathing and circulation, you may be more prone to panic attacks than others for whom stress causes muscular or digestive problems. Many people find that their predisposition to attacks is inherited.

HOW TO COPE WITH A PANIC ATTACK

1 BE RATIONAL Remember that feelings of panic are normal, physical reactions that are exaggerated. They are harmless – nothing worse will happen.

2 STAY WITH THE PRESENT Notice what is happening in your body. Slow yourself down and focus on the word "calm" – but keep going. Relax your muscles and drop your shoulders back so you can breathe deeply.

3 ONLY NOW MATTERS Don't think about what might happen.

4 ACCEPT THE FEELINGS The attack will be over quickly.

5 MEASURE YOUR ANXIETY Grade your anxiety from 10 (high) to 1 (low). Watch your level go down.

6 STAY IN THE SITUATION If you run away or avoid, the situation will be more difficult next time.

7 TAKE SLOW, DEEP BREATHS Concentrate on breathing out.

8 DISTRACT YOURSELF Study your surroundings in great detail.

9 TALK TO SOMEBODY Tell a close friend what you are feeling.

10 CONCENTRATE As the feelings gradually subside, think again about what you were doing before the onset of the attack.

ESSENTIAL **LIFE SKILLS**	CHALLENGING DISTORTED THINKING *See pp.106–107*	LADDERING YOUR THOUGHTS *See p.110*	POSITIVE SELF-STATEMENTS *See p.111*	LEARNING TO RELAX *See pp.128–129*	RELAXED BREATHING *See p.130*

HYPERVENTILATION

*"I first notice my chest tightening. I feel stifled and closed in – as if
I need fresh air. As my breathing becomes faster and
shallower, I worry that I can't get my breath."*

It is natural
to breathe
rapidly when
you feel you
are in danger.

An overload of stresses and demands in your life may make you start to hyperventilate or breathe more quickly than usual. A certain degree of rapid breathing is a natural response to danger, since it ensures that your muscles have enough extra oxygen for "fight or flight." However, prolonged hyperventilation triggered by stress or emotion upsets the balance of gases in the lungs. Too much oxygen and too little carbon dioxide can alter the acidity of the blood, causing dizziness, shaking, tension, or sweating, which may result in an overwhelming feeling of panic. Once you are aware of the symptoms, you may experience more worry and stress, and more hyperventilation, creating a vicious circle. Acute hyperventilation is possibly the cause of panic attacks in seven out of ten people.

Hyperventilation is relatively common, and it is useful to know what action to take if it happens to someone you are with. First, stay calm and gently encourage him or her to use some of the tips listed below. Then comfort the person physically – a hand cupping the back of the neck or an arm around the upper back may help. If he or she becomes emotional, do not argue. Afterward, treat as if for shock with rest and a sweet drink.

CONTROL HYPERVENTILATION

1 RECOGNIZE WARNING SIGNS
Check your breathing at different times of the day, and learn to recognize warning signs such as feeling stifled, fast breathing, and tightness of the chest.

2 RELAX Focus on the word "calm." Drop your shoulders. This stretches the chest and diaphragm muscles outward.

3 BREATHE FROM YOUR STOMACH
Breathe in and out to a slow count of four. Rest your hands, fingertips touching, on your stomach. As you breathe in, they should come apart.

4 LEARN THE "REBREATHING TECHNIQUE" This useful technique involves rebreathing the carbon-dioxide-rich air that you have just breathed out. Cup your hands together and place them over your nose and mouth. Breathe out hard through your mouth and rebreathe the air slowly through your nose. If you can use a paper bag instead of your hands, this gives even better results. Do not repeat this exercise more than four or five times.

ESSENTIAL LIFE SKILLS	RATIONAL THINKING *See pp.104–105*	LADDERING YOUR THOUGHTS *See p.110*	POSITIVE SELF-STATEMENTS *See p.111*	LEARNING TO RELAX *See pp.128–129*	RELAXED BREATHING *See p.130*

OBSESSIVE BEHAVIOR

*"Every time I leave the house, I keep worrying
that I haven't locked the door. I sometimes
end up going back five or six times to check."*

If you tend to be a perfectionist, never happy unless things are just right, you may find you have a tendency to become obsessive in times of extreme personal stress or change. This means that you are prone to intrusive, worrying, repetitive, and often nonsensical thoughts. Sometimes these thoughts may present themselves as a disproportionate fear of illness, such as cancer or AIDS, or a fear of violence: for example, "I'm going to harm somebody." Equally, they may be expressed as doubts: "I've left the oven on" or "Did I lock the door?" In an attempt to neutralize such thoughts, you may also develop ritualistic behavior, or compulsions, such as repeatedly washing your hands, checking, counting, or

hoarding. Sometimes you may have intrusive thoughts that terrify you, such as "I'm going to stab my baby" or "I'm going to kill my father." Try to be rational about these. They are only thoughts, and the risk of translating them into action is almost nonexistent.

If you are frequently troubled by intrusive thoughts, you will often start to avoid situations that might trigger them. Although avoidance may help to reduce your anxiety in the short term, if you do not confront your fears, you may actually become more anxious in the long term.

"I was sure I had cancer and would die."

DEAL WITH OBSESSIONS AND COMPULSIONS

1 WRITE DOWN YOUR THOUGHTS List your most troublesome obsessional thoughts and identify any associated compulsions or rituals.

2 GRADED EXPOSURE List, in order of difficulty, the situations that you tend to avoid, then confront each one separately, starting with the easiest.

3 PREVENT A RESPONSE Learn a relaxation routine (*see pp.128–129*) to help you control your anxiety and prevent any compulsions that might follow.

4 PRACTICE Concentrate on your intrusive thought for as long as possible. Write it down repeatedly and think about it for ten minutes twice a day.

5 THOUGHT STOPPING Put a rubber band around your wrist. Every time you have an unwanted thought, tweak the band, shout "stop" to yourself, and deliberately think about something else. As you improve this technique you will eventually be able to give up the rubber band and change thoughts automatically.

| ESSENTIAL LIFE SKILLS | CONTROLLING PERFECTIONISM *See p.99* | RATIONAL THINKING *See pp.104–105* | CHALLENGING DISTORTED THINKING *See pp.106–107* | LEARNING TO RELAX *See pp.128–129* | RELAXED BREATHING *See p.130* |

FEARS AND PHOBIAS

"Every time I go into a situation where I feel 'trapped' – like an underground train – I feel anxious. I have started to avoid more and more. It's as if my world is shrinking."

The single factor that perpetuates a fear is continuous avoidance.

A phobia is an intense fear of an object or a situation that is out of all proportion to the situation that evokes it. An estimated one in nine people accept mild phobias as a part of life. However, in times of great personal stress, even the mildest phobia can turn into a real and terrifying fear that can lead to hyperventilation and panic attacks. Phobias can be subdivided into three groups:

- SIMPLE PHOBIAS These may be a fear of animals, such as birds, spiders, cats, snakes, mice, or dogs; a fear of nature – for example, heights, darkness, thunder, lightning, water, wind, or death; or a fear of illness or injury, such as vomiting, blood, needles, or hospitals.
- SOCIAL PHOBIAS People suffering from social phobias display an abnormal fear of meeting new people, socializing, eating with others, speaking in public, or criticism.
- AGORAPHOBIA This is a network of fears and avoidances that is associated with a feeling of being trapped, where there is no easy escape to a place of security. People suffering from agoraphobia commonly fear crowded stores, shopping malls, planes, buses, subways, highways, lines, movie theaters, or being a long way from home.

GRADED EXPOSURE
A phobia is an avoidance of a situation, because you imagine your anxiety will rise to unacceptable levels. However, if you progressively confront that fear and stay in the situation, your anxiety will go down. Initially, you will feel anxious, and your anxiety will take time to reduce, but every subsequent time you confront the feared situation, your anxiety is slightly less and returns to normal more quickly. This is the principle of graded exposure or systematic desensitization.

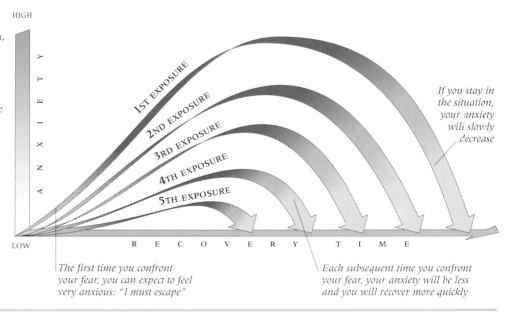

HIGH

ANXIETY

1ST EXPOSURE
2ND EXPOSURE
3RD EXPOSURE
4TH EXPOSURE
5TH EXPOSURE

LOW

RECOVERY TIME

If you stay in the situation, your anxiety will slowly decrease

The first time you confront your fear, you can expect to feel very anxious: "I must escape"

Each subsequent time you confront your fear, your anxiety will be less and you will recover more quickly

Phobic reactions often have their origins in traumatic experiences from the past or in childhood fears that have failed to diminish over time. However, the single main factor that perpetuates a fear or phobia is avoidance.

AVOIDANCE

If you start to avoid certain situations because they make you feel anxious, your anxiety will immediately go down, but only in the short term. Consciously and subconsciously you stamp in the message, "The only way I can cope with this situation is to avoid it." However, the next time you are faced with the same situation, your desire to avoid will be even greater, as you imagine that your anxiety level will go up to an even higher point. What you do not realize is that, if you stay in the situation, after a time your anxiety naturally begins to decrease of its own accord. If you leave the situation quickly or avoid it altogether, you will never find this out.

If it is not tackled, continued avoidance of particular situations can start to interfere with your daily life. One way to control it is deliberately to confront your fear. The next time you are exposed to a situation you have been avoiding for weeks, months, or even years, try to stay in it, however unpleasant it feels. Tell yourself that although you feel a high level of anxiety now, you need to go through this before the anxiety can start to diminish. At the second exposure, your anxiety will be slightly less and will continue to decrease with each successive exposure to the fear. Gradually, it will return to a normal, acceptable level. This is the principle behind the treatment known as graded exposure, or systematic desensitization.

You need to be able to confront your fear before your anxiety level can start to diminish.

CONQUER YOUR FEARS AND PHOBIAS

1 UNDERSTAND YOUR FEAR
Where did it come from? Did you have a bad experience? Were you exposed to people who taught or reinforced this fear and allowed you to avoid it at an early age?

2 WHAT ARE YOU AFRAID OF?
Write down five things that you think will happen if you face your fear.

3 MANAGE YOUR ANXIETIES
Learn some relaxation and distraction techniques, and how to slow down your breathing and challenge irrational thoughts.

4 FACE YOUR PHOBIA Accept that the only way you will overcome your fear is by facing up to it. With time, your fear will gradually lessen.

5 CONSTRUCT A LADDER
List ten situations associated with your phobia that you avoid. Rate each one on a scale of 1–10, where 1 = no anxiety and 10 = high anxiety. Rank the list in order of difficulty, then work up it from the bottom and overcome each stage before moving up. Be aware of your anxiety level gradually falling.

ESSENTIAL LIFE SKILLS	RATIONAL THINKING *See pp.104–105*	CHALLENGING DISTORTED THINKING *See pp.106–107*	LADDERING YOUR THOUGHTS *See p.110*	POSITIVE SELF-STATEMENTS *See p.111*	LEARNING TO RELAX *See pp.128–129*

DEPRESSION

"I don't want to see anybody – what's the point?
No one really wants to see me anyway – and why should they?
I am so miserable. Sometimes I just want to sit and cry."

"I feel as if I am sinking or wallowing in a deep pit."

Most or us are likely to feel depressed at some time in our lives, although some individuals are more vulnerable to depression than others. Symptoms vary, but sufferers often describe depression as a feeling of lethargy, almost like having the flu. It is often likened to being "stuck in a dark tunnel," "in a black pit," or "seeing the world through dark glasses." Depression differs from sadness: it is a state of being emotionally blocked – "feeling dead inside" – whereas sadness is a rich, deep emotion that, even though it hurts, makes us feel alive.

Depression is often caused by a combination of factors. There might be a number of predisposing factors and then several "trigger" factors. The predisposing, or vulnerability, factors might include:

■ BIOLOGICAL FACTORS You may have a bio-chemical vulnerability caused by low amounts of the brain chemicals serotonin and noradrenalin.

■ INABILITY TO EXPRESS FEELINGS You may be prone to depression if you are unable to communicate openly and confidently your thoughts and feelings, especially anger and frustration. Some people say that depression is anger turned inward.

■ LOW SELF-ESTEEM If, as a child, you did not internalize a good feeling about yourself from your parents, you may feel unhappy about who you are and doubt your own self-worth.

■ BELIEFS AND ATTITUDES Certain ways of thinking can predispose you to depression – for example, if you have a perfectionist personality and feel that you have to get everything just right to avoid failure, or if you constantly seek approval and believe "I must work extra hard to prove my worth."

■ SOCIAL MODELING If a role model, such as your mother, was often depressed during your childhood, you may find that as an adult you start to follow the same pattern.

Factors that are known to trigger depression are:

■ TOO MANY DEMANDS You may feel over-whelmed by too much to do and too many people pulling you in different directions.

■ LOSSES Any kind of loss may make you feel depressed. You may be suffering after the loss of a loved one who has recently died, or it could be the loss of a job or

---

SYMPTOMS OF DEPRESSION

- THINKING: poor concentration, poor memory, inability to make decisions, loss of interest, self-criticism, pessimism, preoccupation with self.

- FEELINGS: sadness, low confidence, low pleasure, apathy, guilt, irritability, feelings of unattractiveness, helplessness.

- BEHAVIOR: reduced levels of activity, withdrawal from other people, restlessness, crying, loss of interest in sex, alteration in appetite, disturbed sleep patterns, fatigue, inertia.

retirement. Other losses might include loss of hope, loss of self-image (often after a traumatic event such as a separation or divorce), loss of usefulness (which is common in people who have recently retired), or loss of social support, perhaps as a result of moving to a new home or job.

■ TOO MANY CHANGES If too many life events occur in a very short space of time, this can cause stress and ultimately depression.

UNDERSTAND THE REASONS

Once you are in a depressive phase, it takes time and patience to come out of it. It is not so easy just to "pull yourself together," as some unsympathetic observers may suggest. However, there are steps you can take to "get out of the pit" and feel alive again. First, you need to look at what may be causing your

depression. Do you lack confidence? Do you hide your feelings? Perhaps you are a perfectionist. Second, you need to look at what has triggered your depression. Have you recently suffered a loss, however trifling? Have you had a number of fundamental changes in your life recently? Do you feel you have too much to do? Once you have isolated areas where you feel you might need help, turn to the Life skills section in Part Three (*see pp.78–139*) for specific programs and advice. Remember, a phase of depression can often be a springboard that makes you change your life, so that you end up achieving what you really want.

> A phase of depression can be a springboard that makes you change your life.

OVERCOME YOUR DEPRESSION

1 SET YOURSELF SIMPLE TASKS Even if you feel sluggish and lack motivation, aim to do a simple task each day, such as making a phone call or writing a letter. Although you may find it hard, see it as a start to feeling better.

2 KEEP A DIARY OF YOUR ACTIVITIES At the end of each day, write down what you have done. Rate each activity in terms of how much pleasure it gave you, and deliberately plan to do more of the things you enjoy.

3 CHALLENGE NEGATIVE THOUGHTS Write down your negative thoughts, such as *"I'm a failure"* or *"Nobody likes me."* Identify thinking distortions and challenge them rationally. When they are aired in the cool light of day, many of these will appear ridiculous and unreasonable.

4 TALK TO OTHER PEOPLE Confide in close friends and members of your family. Describe to them how you are feeling. Keep communicating.

5 EXERCISE MORE Try to do more physical exercise, even if it is only a gentle walk or swim. The body produces natural antidepressant hormones (endorphins) during exercise. Absorbing activities such as gardening and reading can help distract your negative thoughts.

6 EXAMINE YOUR GOALS Put aside time to think about the direction in which your life is going. Are you drifting or doing what you really want to do?

ESSENTIAL **LIFE SKILLS**

ASSERTIVENESS *See pp.82–93*

GOAL PLANNING *See pp.96–97*

RATIONAL THINKING *See pp.104–113*

SELF-CARE *See pp.126–139*

IRRITABILITY AND ANGER

"Sometimes I feel so wound up it takes only the smallest thing to go wrong and I explode, regardless of where I am or who I am with. I seem to lose all control."

Your thoughts, not events, lead to anger.

Irritability and anger are the result of an accumulation of stresses or demands, your thoughts and beliefs about the importance of events, your level of physical tension, your tolerance levels, and your learned social skills in handling frustrating situations. Anger is one of the first emotions that you experience as a baby and perhaps the last emotion that you learn to manage effectively. It is a natural emotion borne out of frustration, threat, and hurt, and is a positive and constructive aid to survival. Its function is to provide a vital boost of physical and emotional energy just when you need it most. Anger becomes a problem only when it occurs too frequently, is too intense, lasts too long, or occurs in an inappropriate situation and leads to aggression.

When you get angry, you may think that you just "snap," but the reality is more complex. In fact, your anger is the end result of a subtle chain of observable events. This chain includes an external trigger (something happens), your interpretation of that trigger (the thought or mental statement you make to yourself), and your increased level of physical arousal (tense muscles, rapid heartbeat, fast breathing). You are like an athlete under the starter's gun at the beginning of a race – tense and ready to go. A loud bang in the crowd can trigger a false start in the same way that you may snap at someone with an irritable comment.

In a world full of people with different interests and goals, it is inevitable that there will be frustration from time to time. Your tolerance of frustration is based on what you learned as a child as well as your own genetic and physio- logical makeup. Events and other people do not make you angry – you make yourself angry because of the way you have learned to think and the deep- seated beliefs you hold.

Research suggests that these deep-seated beliefs center around three main rigid beliefs (*see p.109*):

WHAT MAKES YOU ANGRY?

- TRIGGER A small event may tip the balance and become "the last straw."

- TOO MANY DEMANDS You feel tense, stressed, and under pressure due to having too much to do.

- PHYSICAL TENSION Your body is in a state of arousal. You are ready to snap.

- LOW TOLERANCE OF FRUSTRATION You allow little things to get to you.

- LACK OF FLEXIBILITY Your thoughts are too rigid. You often use the words "must,""should," "ought to."

- PESSIMISM You tend to see the bad side. You often use the words "awful" or "horrible" when things go wrong.

- BOTTLING IT UP You find it difficult to express yourself and allow grievances to build up.

- You believe that others should know what you want and treat you in a particular way
- You think, "This is awful, I can't stand it."
- You believe, "Whoever has done this to me should be punished."

The more rigid these beliefs are, the more likely you will experience anger. For example, when stuck in a traffic jam, it is not the traffic jam that annoys you but your expectations that "the traffic should flow smoothly," "It will be awful if I'm late," "I must be there by two o'clock." The more you use "should," "must," "ought to," and "awful," the more likely you are to feel frustrated and irritable

RECOGNIZE AND CHALLENGE ANGER

If you are to manage your anger successfully, you must be able to recognize and alter the chain of events that causes it. By learning to communicate your feelings assertively, you are less likely to let resentments build up and eventually explode. Sometimes, you need to challenge your beliefs and look at them in a different way. If, for example, you become angry every time your manager arrives late for meetings, it may be because you believe that "Philip should always be on time." Try reframing the situation and looking at it more positively, replacing this statement with "Philip is always late because he is so easy going; an advantage of this is that it makes him easy to work for."

Sometimes it helps to identify and write down positive thoughts that can help to reduce frustration and control anger. For example, if you are losing your temper with your children, the following three thoughts or self-statements might help. "This is a challenge," "Stay calm," "She is just a child." Write these thoughts on a card, learn them, and then insert them into your thinking when you feel anger rising. View controlling your temper as a challenge.

Challenge the beliefs that cause your anger.

MANAGE YOUR ANGER

1 OWN YOUR ANGER
Express your feelings openly. Practice saying *"I feel angry because…"*

2 ANTICIPATE THE TRIGGERS
Keep a diary of situations where you feel angry. Record when, where, and what the triggers were. Identify a pattern of factors that might lead up to expressions of anger.

3 PRACTICE A CALMING ROUTINE
Establish a set routine that you can use if you feel yourself getting angry. Step back, grab hold of something, relax to relieve tension, and take a couple of deep breaths before speaking.

4 CHALLENGE RIGID BELIEFS If your own beliefs are at the root of your anger, challenge them. The more rigid they are, the more likely there will be a surge of anger. Examine your "musts," "shoulds," and "ought tos," and your "awfulizing" beliefs.

5 REFRAME Look at a problem from a slightly different point of view, and repeat to yourself a rehearsed self-statement. When you feel frustrated, deliberately insert these statements into your thought processes.

| ESSENTIAL LIFE SKILLS | EXPRESSING YOUR FEELINGS See pp.88–89 | DEALING WITH ANGER See pp.92–93 | CHALLENGING DISTORTED THINKING See pp.106–107 | HOW TO THINK LESS RIGIDLY See p.109 | RELAXED BREATHING See p.130 |

EATING DISORDERS

"I have a love-hate relationship with eating. All I can think about is food. There are days when I eat nothing, but then I secretly binge. I feel constantly guilty."

Diets do not work: establish a healthy eating plan.

Most eating disorders appear to be influenced by cultural factors, such as the modern fashion for a slim figure and the craze for dieting. In an age where male and female models with perfect figures grace all the glossy magazines and movie screens, being the wrong shape can have a devastating effect on self-confidence. As a result, food and eating have become a battleground for many people, especially women, where there are goodies and baddies, good days and bad days. When some people are under stress, their eating problems may become worse and can lead to a more serious condition, such as anorexia (extreme weight loss due to not eating) or obesity (overeating).

It is estimated that 1 in 20 women in the developed world experiences distressing episodes of uncontrolled binge-eating. For some, their concern about their shape and weight drives them to extreme measures such as prolonged fasting, self-induced vomiting, and taking appetite suppressants and unnecessary laxatives. This condition is called bulimia, which literally means "ox hunger."

THE PROBLEMS OF DIETING

The obvious way to achieve the shape you want is to go on a diet. However, despite the amount of time, effort, and commitment expended on them, diets are rarely successful. There is good evidence that dieting places people under physiological and psychological pressure not to eat and paradoxically causes overeating. Dieting leads to mood swings, causes cycles of starving and overeating, upsets appetite, and creates a preoccupation with food. People who replace a pattern of dieting and bingeing with regular meals do not tend to gain weight, and some lose weight.

Eating problems are often triggered by a period of dieting or a stressful phase in which you have too many demands on your time and feel helpless. There

---

EIGHT STEPS TO STOP BINGEING

1 Restrict eating to one or two areas in the house.

2 Do not engage in any other activity while eating, like watching TV or reading.

3 Eat slowly – put your eating utensils down between mouthfuls. Savor the food.

4 Clear up after every meal. Do not leave leftover food lying around.

5 Limit the amount of bingeable food in the house. Don't buy ready-to-eat foods.

6 When shopping, buy only what is on your list. Avoid shopping when hungry.

7 Never eat directly from containers. Put food on a plate.

8 Leave a small amount of food on the plate at the end of every meal.

are also a number of predisposing factors:
- LOW SELF-ESTEEM A low opinion of yourself may be caused by an unhappy childhood during which your parents did not openly express their love for you. Up to one-third of all people who suffer from chronic bulimia report having been sexually abused.
- PERFECTIONISM If your goals are unattainably high, you will never feel content and relaxed.
- SENSE OF USELESSNESS You may be unhappy with your present circumstances but feel powerless to do anything to change them.
- CULTURAL FACTORS Certain eating problems occur only in particular cultures. Bulimia is almost totally confined to women in developed countries where the emphasis is on slimness.

Obsessive eating damages your health; creates shame, guilt, and depression; encourages isolation; and can devastate your social life. The best way of breaking any of these eating disorders is to establish good eating habits with three regularly spaced meals a day, interspersed by light, healthy snacks. Try to include plenty of fresh produce in your daily meal plan, and remember that this is not a diet. Eating regular meals does not make you fat.

Eating regular, balanced meals does not make you fat.

REESTABLISH GOOD EATING HABITS

1 ESTABLISH A MEAL PLAN Work out a sensible eating pattern and keep to it. Eat three meals a day, with two or three light snacks. Do not go for more than three or four hours without food.

2 KEEP A DIARY OF YOUR EATING If you are aware that you have a specific eating disorder, such as bulimia, obesity, or anorexia, write down when, where, and what you eat. Use a new page for each day. Do not abandon your diary even when things go wrong. Look at this record for a pattern, and use it to identify times when you are at your most vulnerable.

3 STOP BINGE EATING Learn to recognize the circumstances that cause you to binge, work out ways of dealing with them so you can prevent the bingeing. Try telling a friend how you feel.

4 STOP DIETING Learn more about healthy eating, particularly the benefits of more fiber and reducing saturated fats. If you narrowly restrict yourself to eating only certain foods, try to broaden your range by gradually and progressively reintroducing avoided foods back into your meal plan. Establish a routine of healthy, regular eating – make it a lifestyle, not a diet.

5 LIST DISTRACTING ACTIVITIES These should be easy, enjoyable activities that remove you from the place of eating (e.g., cycling, gardening, walking, or sports).

6 CHALLENGE IRRATIONAL THINKING Do you consider other people worthy only if they are the right weight and shape? Do you see yourself as a success one day and a failure the next? Challenge this "black-and-white" thinking and look for a middle ground.

7 EXPECT THE OCCASIONAL LAPSE Do not let this demoralize you; it is a part of progress.

ESSENTIAL **LIFE SKILLS**

| CONTROLLING PERFECTIONISM *See p.99* | RATIONAL THINKING *See pp.104–105* | CHALLENGING DISTORTED THINKING *See pp.106–107* | HEALTHY EATING *See pp.134–135* |

EXCESSIVE DRINKING

"Drinking helps me relax, but it has gotten to the stage now where I cannot unwind unless I have a drink. I have recently started drinking a lot more during the day."

Drinking alcohol is not in itself a problem. It is drinking to excess that can be damaging.

Alcohol can give great pleasure and make you feel more relaxed. Drunk in moderation, it helps oil the wheels of communication and can often enhance social events. However, in excess, alcohol is an addictive and potentially dangerous drug. In times of great emotional upset or personal stress it is not uncommon for people to turn to alcohol for comfort and often oblivion. However, although excessive amounts of alcohol can seem to help in the short term, you should try to avoid heavy drinking on a regular basis; it does not help you to tackle the causes of your stress and is likely to create additional, long-term problems.

The risk of becoming dependent on alcohol is high. The two warning signs are firstly when you turn to alcohol as a means of relaxing if you are under pressure, and secondly when you feel you must have a drink. There are no hard-and-fast rules as to how much you need to drink before you can be considered to have

a problem, but, generally, if you often drink on your own, rather than socially or at mealtimes, and if you are regularly drinking more than just a couple of drinks every day, and at unusual times such as during the morning, you should start to take special note and try to cut back.

Women tend to get drunk more easily than men, largely because they are usually smaller than men and weigh less. Women also have more fat reserves and a lower proportion of body weight in the form of water, resulting in a higher concentration of alcohol in their blood. In particular, research suggests that excessive drinking by pregnant women may irreparably harm the developing fetus.

Alcohol is a depressant drug that slows the processes occurring in your brain and dulls your reactions. After several drinks, your thinking becomes muddled, and your coordination is greatly reduced, making you clumsy. For these reasons, it is dangerous to drive or operate machinery after drinking, even if you think you feel normal. Alcohol can seriously affect your judgment, and under its influence, even the most level-headed person can be persuaded to take risks.

IDENTIFY WHY YOU DRINK

Be aware of why you drink alcohol. Add your own reasons for drinking to this list.

- I drink because I am bored
- I drink because it helps me relax
- I drink to gain confidence
- I drink because I feel under pressure
- I drink in social situations

Alcoholic drinks can also affect your mood. Social drinking is traditionally associated with being "merry" or "happy," but if you are drinking because you feel stressed or are repressing feelings or anger, having "one too many" may cause you to turn uncharacteristically aggressive or emotional.

EFFECTS OF ALCOHOL

Besides having serious repercussions on your health and potentially reducing your lifespan, regular heavy drinking can also cause major problems in your family and puts a great strain on relationships. Mood swings and unpredictable, unreliable, and often irresponsible behavior may trigger heated arguments and put family members under great stress. Excessive drinking also affects sleep patterns and often causes you to wake early feeling tired and unrested, frequently with a dull headache and a terrible thirst. If this becomes a normal pattern over a prolonged period, you may start to neglect your appearance and find it difficult to cope with the demands of everyday life at home and at work. This inevitably leads you into a vicious circle of stress, which you need to break.

Under the influence of alcohol you can be persuaded to take foolish risks.

CONTROL YOUR DRINKING

1 MAKE DRINKING RULES Write down basic rules for drinking and stick to them. For example,
• I will not drink alone at home
• I will drink only at mealtimes
• I will stop drinking hard liquor.

2 KEEP A DRINK DIARY Write down how much you intend to drink in a week, then record how much you actually drink. If you feel like a drink, rate the "urge" on a 10-point scale, where 1 is weak and 10 is strong.

3 IDENTIFY VULNERABLE TIMES Use your diary to identify "high-risk" situations and initially avoid them. Become more aware of your drinking patterns. When you feel stronger, go back into high-risk situations, cope by not drinking, and gain confidence.

4 SLOW DOWN AND CUT BACK
• Sip instead of gulp.
• Put the glass down after sips.
• Pace your drinking through the evening – one an hour, or try alternating alcoholic and nonalcoholic drinks.
• If you're thirsty, start with a nonalcoholic drink.
• Always dilute hard liquor.
• In a bar, ask for weaker drinks.
• Keep a supply of nonalcoholic or low-alcohol drinks at home.
• Don't stockpile alcohol.

5 SAY NO Don't let others pressure you into drinking.

6 IMPROVE YOUR LEISURE SKILLS Explore new activities to occupy your time, particularly those that involve exercise and relaxation.

7 RESIST THE URGE Distract yourself – phone a friend, go for a walk, have a bath.

8 CHALLENGE YOUR THOUGHTS Tell yourself "I don't need a drink. I am strong, I can change."

9 EXPECT SETBACKS One setback does not make a failure. Learn from the experience.

ESSENTIAL LIFE SKILLS	SAYING NO *See pp.90–91*	GOAL PLANNING *See pp.96–97*	RATIONAL THINKING *See pp.104–105*	CHALLENGING DISTORTED THINKING *See pp.106–107*	SELF-CARE *See pp.126–139*

SMOKING

"I started smoking when I was still a teenager. It made me feel more confident when I was out with my friends. I regret it now, though. Smoking has cost me my health, yet I can't give it up."

It is never too late to give up smoking.

The nicotine in tobacco has a soothing effect on the nerves, and the act of lighting up a cigarette and holding it in your hand can be a reassuring ritual in times of stress. However, the nicotine, which can seem to have such a pleasant effect, is a powerful and addictive drug that causes long-term damage to the heart and circulatory system; the tar sticks to the windpipe and inside the lungs, causing respiratory illnesses; and the carbon monoxide in the smoke is a poisonous gas. Heavy smoking over a prolonged period can cause strokes, heart disease, bronchitis, cancer, and numerous other fatal illnesses.

Giving up smoking is difficult and takes time and commitment, but it is never too late to try. If you are to stop successfully, you will need a strong will, patience, and support. Choose a relaxed, stress-free time in your life to start your no-smoking campaign, and discuss your goals with family and friends. Ask them to help you if you weaken. As soon as you stop, you should start to feel healthier.

SEVEN STEPS TO STOP SMOKING

1 DECIDE TO STOP List 10 advantages of not smoking, starting with "a longer life." Pin your list on the wall where you can see it every day.

2 CUT DOWN GRADUALLY Work out how much you smoke per day over a week and plan a realistic reduction program. Cut out a certain number of cigarettes per day, starting with the easiest ones. Reduce this each week until you gradually stop.

3 AVOID OBVIOUS TRIGGERS Don't sit in a smoking area or smoky bar. Break old habits – instead of coffee with a cigarette, try tea with a cookie.

4 CHALLENGE YOUR THOUGHTS If you feel like a cigarette, instead of saying, *"I must have a cigarette,"* say to yourself, *"I would like a cigarette but I don't need one."* Run through the reasons why you are trying to break this habit.

5 COLLECT YOUR STUBS IN A JAR Put old cigarette stubs in a small jar with the cap on. When you feel the urge to smoke, remove the cap and sniff the foul odor.

6 SAY "I DON'T SMOKE" Practice in front of a mirror until it becomes easy. Don't say *"I've given up."*

7 TREAT YOURSELF Use the money you have saved by not smoking to buy yourself a gift.

ESSENTIAL **LIFE SKILLS**	SAYING NO *See pp.90–91*	GOAL PLANNING *See pp.96–97*	RATIONAL THINKING *See pp.104–105*	CHALLENGING distorted thinking *See pp.106–107*	SELF-CARE *See pp.126–139*

TRANQUILIZER ADDICTION

"When I first started taking tranquilizers they gave me a wonderful feeling of calm, which greatly helped. But when I tried to stop taking them, I worried that the feelings of anxiety would return."

If you are feeling very stressed, anxious, or depressed following an emotional upset such as a divorce or the death of someone close, you may find that a short course of tranquilizers helps you get through the day. The advantages of taking tranquilizers are that they can make you less anxious in the short term, can help you tackle difficult situations that you might otherwise avoid, and work very quickly, having an effect on the nervous system in about 15 minutes.

The disadvantages are that tranquilizers only mask the symptoms and do not deal with the fundamental causes of anxiety. By taking tranquilizers, you are avoiding coping on your own, which has the effect of eroding your self-confidence. If you take them over a prolonged period, there is a real danger that you may become addicted to the secure, relaxed feeling they give you and find it difficult to cut down or stop. Tranquilizers also have unpleasant physical side effects such as drowsiness, appetite changes, dry mouth, dizziness, and poor coordination, which can start to affect your performance.

From the 1950s to the 1980s tranquilizers were widely overprescribed, and many people found that they had become addicted to them. Today, most doctors agree that treatment with tranquilizers should be limited to the lowest possible dose for the shortest possible time.

WITHDRAW FROM TRANQUILIZERS

1 PICK A POSITIVE TIME IN YOUR LIFE when you are not in the middle of a life crisis to begin your withdrawal program. This might be a weekend or holiday when you feel least stressed.

2 REDUCE THE DOSE GRADUALLY Consult with your doctor and ask his or her advice. It may take a couple of months or longer.

3 PREPARE FOR WITHDRAWAL SYMPTOMS These are not the anxiety symptoms returning, even if they feel quite similar. Learn a relaxation exercise (*see p.129*)

4 BE POSITIVE Cope with the next few days hour by hour. Withdrawal symptoms will not last forever and are not harmful.

5 ESTABLISH YOUR SOCIAL SUPPORT NETWORK Talk with close friends, family, your doctor, and counselor, and let them know what you are experiencing.

6 KEEP BUSY Distract yourself with tasks that take your mind off the stress of withdrawal. Plan enjoyable distracting activities that you can look forward to.

ESSENTIAL LIFE SKILLS	GOAL PLANNING *See pp.96–97*	RATIONAL THINKING *See pp 104–105*	CHALLENGING DISTORTED THINKING *See pp.106–107*	SELF-CARE *See pp.126–139*

SLEEP PROBLEMS

*"I can't sleep. I lie tossing and turning as the day's events
flash through my mind. When I do go to sleep,
I wake up in the early hours, worrying."*

Your body
will take all
the sleep
it needs
unless it
is forcibly
prevented.

A good night's sleep refuels, revitalizes, and reenergizes you, making you feel refreshed, positive, and equipped to cope with the stresses of a normal day. However, a lack of sleep, often called insomnia, has the opposite effect, making you weary, irritable, and less able to tackle difficult situations. This perceived inability to cope is stressful in itself and may lead to more sleepless nights.

Lack of sleep can be distressing. Lying in bed awake, tossing and turning, is frustrating and upsetting. This often happens the day before an important meeting, a long trip, or an exam, when you are particularly aware that you should be relaxed and at your best. For many people, falling asleep is not the problem. You may regularly wake up in the early hours, perhaps to use the bathroom, but then find it impossible to get back to sleep. In the early morning, even the tiniest worries can seem to grow into enormous problems out of all proportion with reality.

EFFECTS OF STRESS ON SLEEP

Insomnia affects most of us at some stage in our lives. It occurs most frequently when extra demands make you feel stressed and under pressure. As part of the "fight or flight" response, increased levels of the hormone adrenalin in your blood make your body become tense and ready for action. You cannot relax properly and this affects your normal sleeping pattern, resulting in a vicious circle where worry about not sleeping makes you more anxious, causing even more worry and less sleep. If you notice this happening, try to break the pattern. Get up and do something different or try to distract yourself.

CAN LACK OF SLEEP HARM ME?

The amount of sleep each of us needs varies greatly between individuals and may well be inherited. On average, adults sleep seven and a half hours each night, although a few people feel fine on four, and others need a full ten hours. People often worry about losing a few nights' sleep, but there is no real danger, since your body will take all the sleep it needs unless forcibly prevented. Experiments on sleep deprivation show that the occasional night of poor sleep may make you feel tired the next day but has little effect on your performance. Two hours of sleep, as long as this occurs on occasional nights only, seems adequate to prevent noticeable effects on thinking tasks. There is therefore no need to worry about sleeping badly the night before an exam or important event.

Our sleep pattern varies at different times of the night. About one-fifth of the time you sleep is spent in light, rapid-eye-movement, or REM, sleep, during which your eyes move quickly from side to side, your brain is very active, you are easily awakened, and you are most likely to dream. During non-REM, or deep, sleep, the brain is less active but there is a great deal of bodily activity, since hormones are released into the bloodstream, and body tissue repairs itself. It is thought that it is more difficult to get back to sleep if your non-REM sleep is broken, than if REM sleep is disturbed.

DREAM-DISTURBED SLEEP
Dreams often reflect events that you have not emotionally processed. If your sleep is often disrupted by dreams, you need to be aware of the thoughts that may be causing them. As soon as you wake up, write down as much of

your dream as you can remember and discuss it with a friend while it is fresh in your mind. In particular, try to recall the feelings your dream aroused and compare the events in the dream with events in your life.

SHOULD I TAKE SLEEPING PILLS?
An occasional sleeping pill taken on your doctor's advice might be useful in the short term, but it is not advisable to take pills regularly and frequently, since they tend to make you tired and irritable the next day and lose their effect quite quickly. It is far more beneficial to attempt to analyze the reasons for your not sleeping so you can tackle the problems. The tips listed below should help you reestablish a normal sleeping routine.

HOW TO ENSURE A GOOD NIGHT'S SLEEP

1 RELAX BEFORE GOING TO BED Take a warm bath, sip a milky drink, or listen to soothing music.

2 AVOID STIMULANTS Cut out tea, coffee, or cola drinks a few hours before retiring. Also avoid spicy food or a heavy meal.

3 MAKE SURE YOUR ROOM IS QUIET Is your bed comfortable? Leave a window open for fresh air.

4 KEEP A REGULAR ROUTINE Go to bed and wake up at the same time every day whether you are tired or not. Resist catnapping during the day.

5 SAVE YOUR BED FOR SLEEP Do not eat, watch TV, or discuss troublesome issues in bed.

6 GET MODERATE EXERCISE Include some exercise in your day, such as swimming or walking.

7 DON'T DRINK TOO MUCH Avoid having to get up and use the bathroom during the night.

8 PLAY DISTRACTING MENTAL GAMES Distract yourself by remembering the names of football teams in the league, people at school, or by counting prime numbers.

9 DO SOMETHING UNSTIMULATING If you have not fallen asleep after half an hour, get up, go to another room, and do something undemanding such as reading or ironing for 10–15 minutes.

10 LEAVE YOUR PROBLEMS BEHIND Before you go to bed, write down your worries on a piece of paper and leave them behind in another room.

11 PROGRESSIVE MUSCLE-RELAXATION EXERCISE As you lie in bed, tighten up muscle groups in the body and slowly relax them (see p.129).

| ESSENTIAL LIFE SKILLS | CHALLENGING distorted thinking See pp.106–107 | DEMOLISH YOUR WORRIES See pp.112–113 | LEARNING TO RELAX See pp.128–129 | RELAXED BREATHING See p.130 | PHYSICAL EXERCISE See pp.132–133 |

CHRONIC FATIGUE

*"I used to be an active person, but now I feel exhausted
all the time. Yet I can't sleep at night. I don't feel motivated to
do anything – I have no energy and constantly feel blue."*

If, as a normally active person, you suddenly lack energy and feel chronically tired or exhausted, you will naturally worry. However, such feelings of fatigue are common and are often brought on by a combination of mental and physical factors such as an accumulation of everyday stresses and a busy lifestyle with too much to do and no time for a good rest. Major life changes, such as moving households or changing jobs, anxiety, failure to get over a viral illness, and even a perfectionist nature can also result in chronic feelings of lethargy. Try to analyze the sources of stress that may lie at the root of your feelings of fatigue, and also work out ways of getting back to normal. If it it not attended to, a lack of energy may erode your ability to cope with further stresses and a spiraling vicious circle can easily become established.

Fatigue syndrome is often characterized by a "seesaw" effect on activity levels where you might do too much one day and too little the next. Doing less may help in the short term, but in the long term inactivity makes you feel more exhausted and lethargic. Learn to pace yourself. Prolonged inactivity leads to sleep problems, loss of motivation, and reduces your physical fitness.

OVERCOME FATIGUE

1 INCREASE YOUR ACTIVITY LEVELS Plan an activity for each day. Start with easy tasks over short periods of time and slowly build up. Pace yourself so you do not overdo it. Keep a diary so that you can monitor progress.

2 CHALLENGE NEGATIVE THINKING Be aware of "all-or-nothing" or "black-and-white" thinking, such as *"I can't do anything today,"* or *"I'll never get any better."*

Challenge such thoughts with more rational, grayish statements, such as *"I need to pace myself today"* and *"I'm slowly making progress."*

3 DON'T DWELL ON HOW YOU FEEL Distract your thoughts. Focus on something different.

4 SLEEP AT REGULAR TIMES Get up and go to bed at the same time each day.

5 IMPROVE YOUR LIFESTYLE Plan a healthy, balanced diet. Eat three times a day, and try to do some physical exercise. Cut out alcohol and smoking; both increase levels of fatigue.

6 EXPECT SETBACKS Accept that relapses are a normal part of progress. It is often said that people suffering from fatigue need to feel worse before they feel better.

ESSENTIAL LIFE SKILLS	GOAL PLANNING *See pp.96–97*	CONTROLLING PERFECTIONISM *See p.99*	CHALLENGING DISTORTED THINKING *See pp.106–107*	PHYSICAL EXERCISE *See pp.132–133*	HEALTHY EATING *See pp.134–135*

LOW SELF-ESTEEM

"Why is it that other people manage to achieve what they want, but whenever I try, it never seems to work out right? I don't like to disturb them for advice – they are all too busy."

Confidence is directly related to your self-esteem, which is the way you feel about yourself and how well you believe you can perform certain tasks. A background of stability and warm relationships, particularly in childhood, helps to boost self-esteem and confidence, but if things go wrong and you feel under stress, confidence can ebb away.

Confidence has a tendency to spiral either upward or downward. If you have a positive attitude, you are likely to perform well, which makes you feel good. Feeling good, in turn, increases your confidence so you can give an even better performance and gain more confidence. Conversely, if your confidence is low, you will be easily discouraged, resulting in a poor performance, which will make you want to avoid the situation. This leads to feelings of failure and lower confidence.

If you are lacking in confidence, begin by looking for small steps you can take to gradually rebuild a feeling of usefulness and effectiveness. Discussing your problems openly with others usually helps.

> *"No one can make you feel inferior without your consent."*
> E. ROOSEVELT

BUILD UP YOUR CONFIDENCE

1 DON'T PUT YOURSELF DOWN Use the word "I" to ask for what you want and learn to be assertive.

2 PRACTICE Confidence is gained through practice. The first time you ride a bicycle you fall off, but with practice you can become as good a cyclist as anyone.

3 ACT THE PART Try to act out the posture, actions, thoughts, and speech of a confident person.

4 LOOK THE PART Treat yourself to some new clothes or a new hairstyle to make you feel good.

5 VISUALIZE YOUR ACHIEVEMENTS Mentally rehearse something you plan to achieve. Focus on how you might look, feel, and even what you taste, smell, and hear.

6 LEARN FROM YOUR MISTAKES If you make a mistake, rather than criticize yourself, learn from it.

7 DON'T BLAME YOURSELF Ignore or challenge that inner critical voice: *"I did it wrong, I'm useless."* Tell yourself positively, *"Next time I will get it right."*

8 MIX WITH PEOPLE WHO MAKE YOU FEEL GOOD Avoid friends who undermine your confidence.

9 TREAT YOURSELF Don't punish yourself. Learn to treat yourself and give yourself rewards.

ESSENTIAL
LIFE SKILLS

RATIONAL
THINKING
See pp.104–105

CHALLENGING
DISTORTED THINKING
See pp.106–107

COMMUNICATING
IN RELATIONSHIPS
See pp.116–117

SELF-CARE
See pp.126–139

HEADACHES AND MIGRAINES

"If I've had a stressful day – particularly if I miss a meal or eat late – my head starts to ache. At the end of the day, I can feel it throbbing."

Stress is a principal trigger for headaches.

Most of us suffer from headaches from time to time, but if they occur regularly, they can start to affect the way we think and behave, making us feel subdued, and anxious to discover the cause. When you are over-worked or under stress, you are likely to tense up the muscles in your neck, head, and shoulders. Classic signs are hunched shoulders and furrowed brows. When you are unable to relax these taut muscles – particularly the frontalis muscles in the forehead and the temporalis muscles on the sides of the head – you are most likely to develop what is called a tension headache, characterized by an aching sensation and pressure. A second type of headache, or migraine, is often characterized by a throbbing pain, occasionally on one side of the head. Sometimes sufferers will notice visual and sensory disturbances before the onset of the headache. Recent research into migraine headaches suggests that pain is caused as a result of the stress hormone serotonin being released into the bloodstream making blood vessels in the brain swell.

Besides the purely physiological causes of headaches, stress, whether due to overwork, worry, exhaustion, or problems in the home or family, is acknowledged as a principal trigger. Some experts estimate that as many as nine out of ten headaches are stress-related.

However, there are other important factors that may interact with or increase stress, such as certain foods, lack of food, hormonal changes, changeable environment, muscle tension, sleep problems, or overexertion. These triggers usually act in combination with each other, building up gradually over a period of time, eventually triggering a headache. Rather than asking yourself "What triggers my headache?" a more useful question is "How many triggers do I need before I develop a headache?"

POSSIBLE CAUSES OF HEADACHES

- CERTAIN FOODS These include chocolate, cheese, tea, coffee, colas, alcohol, dairy products, fried food, citrus fruits, nuts.

- LACK OF FOOD Missing meals affects blood sugar levels. Always eat breakfast. Do not replace meals with sugary snacks.

- MUSCLE TENSION Hunching over a desk, screen, or steering wheel can tense up the muscles in the shoulders, neck, and eyes.

- HORMONAL CHANGES Oral contraceptive pills, menstruation, and menopause often cause headaches in women.

- CHANGES IN SLEEPING PATTERN Too much or too little sleep can cause headaches.

- ENVIRONMENTAL CONDITIONS Avoid extremes of temperature, flickering or bright lights, loud noise, or stuffy rooms.

- HARD PHYSICAL EXERCISE If you are out of shape, overexertion can be a trigger.

Keep a diary or record of when headaches occur to see if there is a pattern. Record the date, time, symptoms, what happened just before the symptoms, potential triggers, what you ate, whether you felt stressed, and what treatment was used and whether it was effective. You may find that you develop a headache if you miss a meal. If you often have a headache on the weekends, it might be due to family stress or because you drink more alcohol on Friday nights. Frequent headaches on Monday morning may be the result of stress at work. Study your list of potential triggers from your headache diary, and, if possible, try to cut out suspected triggers one at a time. If you think that food is a trigger, cut the food items listed at left from your diet for a three- to four-week period and see if there is a difference. Then gradually reintroduce the foods one at a time and notice if any changes take place.

There are a number of other background factors that can increase the risk of developing a headache:

- POOR EYESIGHT
A weakness in one or more eye muscles may be causing you to contract other muscles in an effort to maintain normal binocular vision. The resulting strain can cause a headache. Do you need an eye test?
- SINUSITIS If your head feels chronically heavy and stuffed up, it may be the result of infected sinuses or you may be suffering from nasal congestion.
- HIGH BLOOD PRESSURE The cause of your headaches may be high blood pressure. Have you had your blood pressure checked?
- GENETIC LINK A tendency to suffer from headaches often runs in families. Do, or did, your parents often have headaches?

Are your headaches caused by certain foods?

RELIEVE HEADACHES

1 LEARN A RELAXATION TECHNIQUE Alternately tense and relax selected groups of muscles in the head, neck, and shoulders to ease the pain (see pp.128–129).

2 MASSAGE AND MOVEMENT Gently press your temples with your fingertips, squeeze the base of the neck, and rest your palms on your closed eyes. Stretching your neck muscles to soothing music also helps.

3 RELAX YOUR MUSCLES A hot-water bottle on your neck, a warm bath, a warm towel on your head or face, or a cold washcloth or cold compress can all help to relax muscles.

4 RETREAT Lie down and relax in a peaceful dark room.

5 CHECK YOUR DIET Cut out any foods you suspect of triggering your head pain.

6 EAT REGULAR MEALS Avoid skipping meals since this causes low blood sugar levels and headaches. A high-fiber snack can help, but avoid sugary snacks, since they temporarily raise then lower blood sugar levels.

7 SCENTS AND SALTS Lavender oil, or other aromatic oils, gently massaged into your temples or sprinkled on your pillow at night can help alleviate tension.

| ESSENTIAL **LIFE SKILLS** | LEARNING TO RELAX *See pp.128–129* | RELAXED BREATHING *See p.130* | REDUCING ENVIRONMENTAL STRESS *See p.131* | HEALTHY EATING *See pp.134–135* |

HIGH BLOOD PRESSURE

*"When I was told I had high blood pressure I couldn't understand why.
I know I'm not in very good shape, but I've always been active, and
driven myself very hard. I'll have to be more careful from now on."*

"I never knew I had high blood pressure."

High blood pressure, or hypertension, is likely to affect at least one in seven of us at some time in our lives. The pressure under which the heart pumps blood around the body is regulated by the size of the blood vessels, or arteries, through which it passes. High blood pressure occurs when these arteries become clogged with fatty deposits, which make them narrower. The effect is a little like what happens if you pinch a hose. The flow of water slows down, and the pressure builds up. Blood pressure does not increase overnight but usually builds up over a period of years. However, since there are few symptoms until it becomes critical, it is important to be aware of ways of regulating it. The major risks for high blood pressure are obesity, drinking too much alcohol, a high-fat and high-salt diet, smoking, lack of exercise, and stress.

The people at greatest risk of developing high blood pressure are usually energetic, hard-driving, competitive, and time-conscious personalities who lead a fast, stressful life and tend to become easily frustrated and angry. If you recognize these traits in yourself, you should try deliberately to change your behavior and slow yourself down.

By planning a healthy lifestyle now, you can greatly reduce the risk of developing high blood pressure and consequently of heart disease in later life.

PREVENT HIGH BLOOD PRESSURE

1 KEEP YOUR WEIGHT DOWN Eat a sensible diet of fresh produce.

2 IMPROVE YOUR DIET Drink less coffee, tea, and cola and cut down on sugar-rich foods and dairy products. Reduce your intake of salt, and try to limit your consumption of alcohol.

3 STOP SMOKING Tobacco temporarily raises blood pressure.

4 GET REGULAR GENTLE EXERCISE Try to walk as much as possible instead of using a car.

5 SLOW DOWN Find time to relax and adopt a calm approach.

6 DO RELAXATION EXERCISES Research has shown that regular use of progressive muscle relaxation exercises (*see p.129*) reduces high blood pressure.

7 CHECK YOUR BLOOD PRESSURE If you are over 35 years old, have a checkup every three years.

ESSENTIAL **LIFE SKILLS**	REDUCING HURRY SICKNESS *See pp.102–103*	LEARNING TO RELAX *See pp.128–129*	RELAXED BREATHING *See p.130*	PHYSICAL EXERCISE *See pp.132–133*	DEVELOPING HOBBIES AND INTERESTS *See p.136*

IRRITABLE BOWEL SYNDROME

*"I feel uncomfortable and have frequent bouts of diarrhea.
I worry about it rather obsessively and I don't like to go
anywhere if I can't be near a bathroom."*

Irritable bowel syndrome, often called simply IBS, is a malfunction of the way in which the contents of the digestive system – the food you eat – moves through your intestine. This malfunction is closely related to the way your intestine reacts both to diet and the stresses of everyday life. Stress affects everyone in different ways. Some people develop problems with their breathing or circulation, but for people who suffer from IBS the bowel is the weak link. The symptoms of IBS are unpleasant and include abdominal pain, bouts of diarrhea and constipation (these are often erratic and unpredictable, alternating from one to the other), a bloated, distended abdomen, frequent gas, and mucus in the stools.

IBS is a common complaint and affects between 8 and 17 percent of the population of most developed countries. Extremes range from healthy individuals who accept their symptoms and continue as normal, to others who are scared to move far from the toilet, and whose digestive system has become the focal point of their lives.

More people suffer from IBS than is generally realized.

HOW TO MANAGE IBS

1 LEARN A RELAXATION TECHNIQUE Alternately tensing and relaxing selected groups of muscles (*see p.129*) can help to reduce IBS.

2 EAT REGULAR, HEALTHY MEALS Never hurry your food; eat slowly. Take time for a leisurely breakfast. Eat high-fiber, low-fat foods such as wholegrain bread, fruit and vegetables, and dried fruit and legumes, such as beans and lentils.

3 DON'T AVOID Try not to avoid stressful situations, as this will only make your symptoms worse in the long run. Watch out for the vicious spiral of worrying thoughts and avoidance, leading to worse symptoms.

4 KEEP PHYSICALLY ACTIVE Take your mind off your symptoms by doing exercises, especially those that strengthen the abdominal muscles, such as sit-ups.

5 GAS Try peppermint oil capsules or minty candies as a remedy to help relieve gas.

6 DIARRHEA Before each meal drink a teaspoonful of cider vinegar in a glass of water.

7 CONSTIPATION Drink plenty of fluids. Eat a high-fiber breakfast and allow yourself 10–15 minutes in the bathroom. Don't strain. Don't worry if you can't go.

ESSENTIAL
LIFE SKILLS

DEMOLISH
YOUR WORRIES
See pp.112–113

LEARNING
TO RELAX
See pp.128–129

PHYSICAL
EXERCISE
See pp.132–133

HEALTHY
EATING
See pp.134–135

SOURCES *of* STRESS

WHAT CAUSES YOU STRESS?

Look down the following list and circle the major life events you have encountered over the past year. The accumulation of significant life events in any one year increases your vulnerability to stress-related illness.

SCORING

The following scores are loosely based on research carried out by Holmes and Rahe (1967), who studied the relationship between life events and stress-related health problems.

1	Death of your spouse or life partner	100	17	Unexpected accident or trauma	45
2	Divorce or separation	75	18	Changes at work/increased demands	35
3	Major illness or injury	70	19	Outstanding personal achievement or promotion	35
4	Loss of a job	70	20	Caring for an elderly or sick relative or friend	35
5	Problems with the law/imprisonment	70	21	Problems with relatives, family, friends, or neighbors	35
6	Death of someone close	60	22	Financial worries	35
7	Marital reconciliation	60	23	Examinations, extra study, or having to speak in public	30
8	Retirement	60	24	Changes in social activities	30
9	Illness in your immediate family	50	25	Changes in recreational activities	30
10	Marriage or moving in with partner	50	26	Children going or "growing" away	30
11	Moving house or major renovation	50	27	Premenstrual syndrome or menopause	30
12	Gaining a new family member – through birth or adoption	50	28	Starting a new relationship	30
13	Pregnancy	45	29	Going on vacation	20
14	Increase in the number of arguments or disagreements with partner	45	30	Family gatherings, Christmas	20
15	Large mortgage, loan, or debt	45		**TOTAL SCORE**	
16	Changing jobs or a new job	45			

INTERPRETING YOUR SCORE

Add up all your scores to find your total. This will give you an approximate measure of how many life changes you have experienced recently and how vulnerable you are to stress-related problems.

Over 280 High vulnerability
You have suffered an unusually high number of stressful life events over the last year, which greatly increases your risk of developing stress-related illnesses. However, illness is not an inevitable result of change. Your personality and ability to cope largely determine how well you react. By improving your life skills, you can be prepared to cope with difficult life events.

130–280 Moderate vulnerability
You have experienced a number of stressful events over the past year, which could increase your risk of stress-related illness. The more you know about these life events and understand the effect they are likely to have on you, the better you will be able to prepare yourself in advance for similar events in the future.

Below 130 Low vulnerability
You have experienced few stressful events over the past year and your life appears to be relatively settled, causing little risk of stress-related illness. However, if you are aware of how you may be affected by major life events, you can ensure that you are well prepared for future changes.

HOW YOU ANSWERED THE QUESTIONS

Stress is not inevitable. It depends to some extent on your perception of an event, what it means to you, and your abilities to cope. If you have circled a life event, refer to the list below and go to the pages given alongside the question number. The pages in Part Two give information and short-term advice on coping with particular life events and how to perceive them. Then turn to Part Three where you will find useful programs to help improve your life skills so you are able to anticipate and cope when these major life events occur.

1 BEREAVEMENT AND LOSS *pp.64–65*
2 SEPARATION AND DIVORCE *pp.58–59*
3 LIVING WITH PAIN *p.57* ACCIDENTS AND TRAUMA *pp.66–67*
4 LIFE WITHOUT WORK *pp.76–77*
5 CHANGE *pp.46–47*
6 BEREAVEMENT AND LOSS *pp.64–65*
7 EXTRAMARITAL AFFAIRS *p.61* IMPROVING RELATIONSHIPS *pp.114–125*
8 LIFE WITHOUT WORK *pp.76–77*
9 LIVING WITH PAIN *p.57* ACCIDENTS AND TRAUMA *pp.66–67*

10 COMMITTING TO A PARTNER *pp.48–49*
11 CHANGE *pp.46–47*
12 BECOMING A PARENT *pp.50–51* FAMILIES AND CHILDREN *pp.52–53*
13 BECOMING A PARENT *pp.50–51*
14 IMPROVING RELATIONSHIPS *pp.114–125*
15 FINANCIAL DIFFICULTIES *p.69*
16 WORK STRESS *pp.73–75*
17 ACCIDENTS AND TRAUMA *pp.66–67*
18 WORK STRESS *pp.73–75*
19 CHANGE *pp.46–47*
20 CARING FOR THE ELDERLY *pp.70–71*

21 IMPROVING RELATIONSHIPS *pp.114–125*
22 FINANCIAL DIFFICULTIES *p.69*
23 EXAM STRESS *p.68* PUBLIC SPEAKING *p.72*
24 CHANGE *pp.46–47* EXPANDING YOUR CIRCLE OF FRIENDS *p.137*
25 CHANGE *pp.46–47* DEVELOPING HOBBIES AND INTERESTS *p.136*
26 ADOLESCENCE *pp.54–55*
27 PREMENSTRUAL SYNDROME *p.56*
28 IMPROVING RELATIONSHIPS *pp.114–125*
29 HOLIDAY STRESS *p.62*
30 HOLIDAY STRESS *p.62*

CHANGE

*"When we move away, it will be like leaving
part of my life behind. I hope I will be as happy in
the new house as I have been here."*

Learn to accept change as a challenge.

Changes, both big and little, sudden and gradual, affect your life from the moment you are born. You learn to cope with small, everyday changes, but major life events can be stressful, because they disturb your routine and cause upheaval. Some changes, like moving into a new house or changing a job, are planned and can, to some extent, be controlled. However, other major events – for example, the break-up of a long-term relationship or sudden ill health – cannot usually be predicted and are beyond your control.

It is widely recognized that if several of these life events, either planned or unpredicted, occur within a short period of time, you may find it difficult to cope and will be more prone to suffer symptoms of stress.

Your normal behavior is based on the picture or mental map you have of your own personal world.

If a major change occurs in your life, such as getting married or the death of someone close – a parent, child, or partner – it means you have to rearrange the map or rewire your internal circuits. This process of change is called adjustment.

LEARNING TO ADJUST

As you adjust to change you can expect to experience feelings of loss, grief, and remorse about the past and what you are letting go, as well as uncertainty and self-doubt about the unknown future and what you are taking on. If you are to cope with a major change in your life, you must be prepared to replace old habits and learn new, appropriate behaviors. You also need to expect to experience emotional ups and downs, which occur as periods of excitement are followed by periods of calm and returning to routine.

If you have a sense of challenge and see change rather than stability as the normal course of life, research indicates that you are

---

HOW DO YOU VIEW CHANGE?

*Think about one area of change in your
life at the moment, then answer the
following questions to find out more
about how you view change.*

- Do you see this change as a challenge or something to avoid?

- What are the obvious advantages?

- What are the obvious disadvantages?

- What are the aspects of the change that make you feel threatened?

- What is the worst possible outcome?

- Can you foresee any long-term effects or opportunities that may result from this change?

- How does the change affect people around you?

- What can you do now to make the change better?

---

less likely to be adversely affected by stressful life events. It is also likely that the more changes you have had to cope with in the past, the more confident you will be at coping with changes in the future.

ACCEPTING CHANGE

Not being able to accept change can lead to emotional problems of depression, anger, resentment, or the inability to forgive. You may find yourself harking back to "life as it was," rather than accepting "life as it is," or thinking "if only" thoughts, rather than accepting "what is." It takes time to adjust to change, and the process is usually slow and gradual. However, in the constantly changing world in which we live, being able to accept change is an essential life skill. Italian saint Francis of Assisi's "Serenity Prayer," written about 700 years ago, captures the essence of this skill – "God, grant me the strength to change that which I need to change, the patience to accept that which I cannot change, and, above all, the wisdom to know the difference."

It is better to plan and be prepared for major life changes and to ensure that they are spread out over time. This allows you time for adjustment, avoids high levels of stress, and means that if an unexpected, uncontrollable event does occur, you are better able to deal with it.

> Most people resist change, but it's the only thing that brings progress.

PREPARE YOURSELF FOR CHANGE

1 DEVELOP A POSITIVE ATTITUDE Examine your attitude toward change. Try to see it as an opportunity and a challenge that will make you a stronger and better person.

2 FIND OUT AS MUCH AS YOU CAN The more information you have about the change, the more prepared you will be to deal with it, and therefore the less likely you will be to worry. Take time to think the whole matter over in a structured way, rather than worrying about details.

3 EXPRESS YOUR FEELINGS Own up to your fears and excitement about the change both to friends and to yourself. Avoid thoughts based on "shoulds," such as "I should be used to this by now."

4 DEVELOP A PLAN OF ACTION Ask yourself how you can improve the situation. Look for potential losses and gains, then look at ways of maximizing the gains and minimizing the losses. Try to visualize the result you want to achieve, then work out what you need to do to get there.

5 TAKE CARE OF YOUR HEALTH It is important to eat well during periods of change. Get plenty of exercise.

6 RALLY YOUR SUPPORT NETWORK Tell your friends and family how you feel about the change.

7 DON'T TAKE ON TOO MUCH Learn how to delegate and say no to extra daily commitments.

8 RELAX Take time out to get away from the situation and allow for emotional repair.

ESSENTIAL **LIFE SKILLS**

ASSERTIVENESS *See pp.82–93*

MANAGING YOUR TIME *See pp.94–103*

RATIONAL THINKING *See pp.104–113*

SELF-CARE *See pp.126–139*

COMMITTING TO A PARTNER

"There is so much to consider. Do we both want children, where will we live, can we afford to buy a house, should we get married or just live together? It's a hundred decisions in one."

It is important to discuss your long-term goals.

Falling in love and deciding to live with someone, and perhaps get married, although happy and exciting events, create enormous changes and stresses in your life. You must adapt to being part of a couple and learn to share yourself and your life with another person whose views and feelings you need to consider as well as your own. The decision to make your relationship long term or to get married cannot be taken lightly, since it irredeemably affects the future course and happiness of your life. Even planning for a wedding itself can be a time of difficult decisions. As with any major life event, stress levels can be greatly reduced by considering as many of the issues involved in the decision process as possible.

In any relationship, there is more than one type of love. Initially there are the feelings of passion, thrill, and romance associated with falling in love, followed by the more down-to-earth, stable feelings that you expect to develop in a strong, long-term relationship. The initial romantic love is wonderful, but it will not last forever, just as the feelings of euphoria produced by drink or drugs soon wear off. Unfortunately, some people become addicted to the sensations of this first love and are constantly searching for it, unable to settle down into a stable relationship. For this reason, it is not usually a good idea to make long-term plans too early in a relationship when you are still feeling intoxicated. Give your love time to prove itself. It is essential that as a couple you have withstood the test of whether you can handle problems together before making a life commitment.

Once some of the initial magic has worn off, any relationship should have a number of essential ingredients if it is to last. You and your partner should genuinely like and respect each other

HOW COMPATIBLE ARE YOU?

These questions cover issues that you and your partner need to confront before committing to a long-term relationship. Answer them separately. Then compare and discuss your responses.

- Do you genuinely like your partner? If you weren't lovers, could you be friends?

- Can your partner make you laugh?

- What do you respect about your partner?

- What similar interests do you enjoy?

- Do you feel sexually attracted to your partner?

- Are you both able to express your feelings and accept constructive criticism?

- How do you see your life together in five, ten, and twenty years' time?

- How do you see your different roles?

- Do you want children; if so, when?

- When things go wrong, how do you react?

and share a sense of humor to help you through any difficult times. Openness and a willingness to negotiate and compromise are also important. Above all, you should be sure you are compatible as a couple, both temperamentally and emotionally. The four most important criteria for compatibility are:
- shared goals, values, and long-term ideals
- common interests and similar backgrounds
- mutual physical attraction
- complementary personalities. For example, if you are outgoing, spontaneous, and occasionally frivolous, and your partner is perhaps more shy and retiring but is steady and reliable, you each give each other qualities that you individually lack. Your two halves make a stronger whole.

The success of any marriage or long-term relationship can be affected by a number of established risk factors, which it is helpful to be aware of. These include marrying on the rebound or as a way of escaping from difficulties in your present life. Marriages are statistically less likely to succeed if either of you is under 19, if there is more than ten years between you, or if you have been together for less than nine months. Finally, it is rarely wise to marry because of a premarital pregnancy.

There is no perfect harmony in marriage, only a series of adjustments.

DISCOVER HOW WELL YOU KNOW EACH OTHER

Try out the following exercises with your partner. If you can both understand and accept each other's views, you are less likely to suffer stress within your relationship.

1 DO YOU HAVE SHARED VALUES? Rank the following values and activities in terms of how important they are to you. Guess the order of each other's list.
- Religion
- A loving relationship
- Hobbies
- Children
- Money
- Creativity
- Work
- Education
- Travel
- Environment
- Music
- Politics
- Friends
- Health
- Humor
- Sexual intimacy
- Sports
- Food

2 WHAT MAKES YOU ANGRY? Pick out the top five things on the following list that are likely to make you angry. Try to guess each other's top five.
- Stupidity
- Lack of money
- Politics
- Environment issues
- Being ignored
- Being lied to
- Being cheated
- Lack of freedom
- Criticism
- Lack of consideration for others
- Cool treatment
- Violence
- Racial issues
- Family
- Rudeness
- Cruelty

3 SEE THE OTHER POINT OF VIEW For five minutes tell your partner how you think he or she sees you. Discuss points that you think your partner finds irritating and would like to change. Switch roles and discuss whether you think you got it right.

4 I LIKE IT WHEN… Draw up a list of things you like your partner to do as well as things you like doing together. Compare lists and choose the things you want to continue.

ESSENTIAL **LIFE SKILLS** | EXPRESSING YOUR FEELINGS *See pp.88–89* | GOAL PLANNING *See pp.96–97* | IMPROVING RELATIONSHIPS *See pp.114–115* | COMMUNICATING IN RELATIONSHIPS *See pp.116–117*

BECOMING A PARENT

"We don't regret it, but ever since she was born it's been a constant round of feeding, washing, changing diapers, people calling round – we hardly have time for each other any more."

Parenting is a skill that has to be learned.

Deciding to have children can be a source of stress for some couples. Timing is often an important factor. At an early stage in your relationship, you may think of children as a life sentence, narrowing your horizons; however, as you mature, you may see parenting as a way of broadening horizons. Your reasons for having children might include a desire to give life a sense of purpose, a need to have someone to love, or boredom with your present situation. Reasons for not wanting children might include not wanting change, a fear of commitment, your own bad experiences as a child, or a fear of not being a good enough parent.

Although having a child is generally an exciting time, it is helpful if you and your partner are both aware of the possible problems and disadvantages. First, once you have made a decision to have children, there are two popular myths about parenting, which need to be exploded:
■ Parents always feel happy and positive about bringing up their child. If you are feeling negative, there is a danger that you might think, "I shouldn't feel like this, there must be something wrong with me."
■ We are all natural parents. The skills of parenting are learned. If you have looked after younger brothers and sisters, you may well have an advantage, however, in many cases, you will be learning "on the job." You are bound to feel confused at times and should expect to make mistakes. Do not be too hard on yourself, and avoid feeling guilty, as this only adds to the stress.

EFFECTS ON YOUR RELATIONSHIP

As soon as your baby is born, your lives will change. You can expect to have less sleep with consequent tiredness, less money, less time for going out or relaxing, extra work, and less sex. Quite suddenly, as the baby becomes the center of attention, the whole balance of the relationship must change. This might mean that if you are the mother, who has been the important one for the past nine months, you find you suddenly receive less attention. Similarly, if you are the father, you may feel neglected as your partner plows all her emotional energy and effort into your child. A baby also changes the balance

---

DISCOVER YOUR FEELINGS

Use the following headings to help you compile a list of the changes that your baby will bring, or has brought to your relationship. Discuss each point on the list with your partner.

• Work	• Social life	• Sex life
• Time	• Finances	• Relationship
• Energy levels	• Feelings about self	• Outside interests

---

of the relationship in that it bonds you and your partner together with a sense of shared duty and responsibility. As a woman, you now have a baby who is totally dependent on you, and as a man, you may feel that your new responsibilities as a father encourage you to adopt a less carefree attitude.

DEMANDS OF PARENTING

Just after your baby is born, you may feel, as a couple, that you are caught in the crossfire of a multitude of often conflicting demands. As a mother, you need to attend to your child, who needs food, comfort, diaper changes, baths, stimulation, and sleep. As a father, you need to feel involved, to have a role, and to receive some attention from your partner. As a couple, you may be inundated with calls and visits from friends and extended family offering help and advice, yet you need to spend time together to talk, be intimate, and have fun. It is clearly impossible to respond to all these different needs.

Rather than trying and failing, accept at the outset that at times, somebody is going to feel left out. After the birth of a baby, up to 30 percent of women feel low. Known as postpartum depression, this condition is often said to be the result of hormonal and chemical imbalances. However, this is usually only part of the story. Lack of self-confidence, worries about the baby, lack of support from partner and friends, exhaustion, and loneliness are all important factors.

If you suffer from postpartum depression you probably feel very irritable and depressed. Be honest about expressing your needs – say what is getting you down. Try to give yourself some time off from the baby and make contact with other mothers in the area.

"We weren't prepared for the way in which the baby seems to control our lives."

HOW TO ADAPT TO LIFE WITH A NEW BABY

1 EXPRESS YOUR FEELINGS OPENLY
Don't bottle up your feelings and thoughts. Talk to your partner and encourage each other to talk and practice listening.

2 GIVE EACH OTHER TIME OFF
Looking after a baby full time can be exhausting. Take turns at jobs like changing diapers so each of you can relax.

3 JOIN A BABY GROUP Make contact with other parents of young children, with whom you have something in common.

4 TAKE UP OUTSIDE INTERESTS
Set aside time for hobbies and interests that you enjoyed before the baby was born. Encourage your partner to do the same. Take turns looking after the baby.

5 PLAN EVENINGS OUT TOGETHER
Find a good babysitter and plan regular outings together without the baby, so you can relax and talk to each other without being disturbed.

6 UNPACK GUILT Watch out for, and challenge, *"I should,"* or *"I ought to"* statements and the guilt they often engender.

ESSENTIAL
LIFE SKILLS

ASSERTIVENESS
See pp.82–93

GOAL
PLANNING
See pp.96–97

DELEGATION
See pp.100–101

HOW TO THINK
LESS RIGIDLY
See p.109

IMPROVING
RELATIONSHIPS
See pp.114–125

FAMILIES AND CHILDREN

*"We are constantly having to adapt to each stage our children
go through as they grow up from babies, through temper
tantrums, to starting school."*

A loved child
is likely to be
an emotionally
stable adult.

When you have children, you move from being a couple to being a family, and relationships inevitably change. Your relationship with your partner changes to make space for the child. Your parents take on a different role and become grandparents. You may feel closer to your parents as you experience situations you recognize from your own childhood. You may ask yourself, "How did my mother do this with me?" Each stage of your child's development brings a different set of challenges and stresses.

Most parents want to provide the right family environment for their children to grow up into healthy, happy, positive people. A certain amount of stress can be created by the worry "Am I doing the right thing?" There is no absolute right and wrong, but research and clinical experience suggest that there are specific ingredients for a healthy family life. Perhaps the two most important factors that you can give a child are:

- He or she grows up feeling loved for who he or she is, not what he or she does
- He or she can communicate openly and directly, expressing the whole array of human emotions. For this to happen, you need to be aware of how a child develops emotionally.

A baby starts out as a mass of pre-programmed impulses and responses, and gradually learns to gain greater control. The child initially learns that he or she is separate, or different, from the environment. He or she learns a sense of "I" or "me." Then the child learns "effectiveness," or the simple rule that, "I can have an effect on the people around me. If I cry somebody will come and feed or cuddle me." The child begins to build up deep-seated beliefs in terms of how effective he or she is, and how consistent and friendly the outside world is. Gradually, he or she begins to understand the rules of everyday life and grasps an appreciation of the concepts of right and wrong. Hopefully, the child also internalizes the deep-seated belief that, "I am a lovable person," irrespective of what I do." For some

TIPS FOR HEALTHY FAMILY LIFE

- Communicate in a straightforward, direct, open, and honest way.

- Accept all feelings and emotions as natural, but expect members to learn control.

- Encourage an atmosphere of fun and enjoyment backed by mutual support.

- Show children authority, but discuss issues with them democratically.

- Do not force children into set "molds," but appreciate them for who they are.

- Encourage commitment to the family, with an ability to develop outside interests.

- Share parental power and swap roles, rather than one parent rigidly dominating.

children this belief may be conditional or have strings attached and evolve into, "I am lovable if I am good or successful." This belief can sometimes create problems in adult life as the person becomes "driven" to be successful or is overly conforming in an attempt to be good.

At the age of about two years, children are prone to temper tantrums – "the terrible twos." Your child might scream, shout, and become puce with rage, which can be distressing for you as parents. You might think incorrectly that you are at fault. Your child is going through a normal stage, where he or she is learning to gain some control over emotions and learning about the acceptable limits of behavior. Parents need to provide these limits and boundaries, and to be firm and consistent. The force of a temper tantrum is a measure of the child's strength of character and self-will, and the way in which you respond is important in shaping his or her emotional development. A very severe, disapproving parental response, which "crushes" this display of emotion, may leave the child unable or unwilling to express similar emotions in the future. At the other extreme, a mixed or ambiguous response, or no response, may leave the child insensitive or unaware of the needs of others. As your child starts to understand the rules and gains greater control, temper tantrums should become less frequent.

Temper tantrums are a normal part of every child's development.

CONTROL TEMPER TANTRUMS

1 DON'T TAKE THE BLAME Keep in your mind that this is a normal phase and not your fault.

2 BE CONSISTENT BUT REASSURING Do not be blackmailed by tantrums. Show your child that a tantrum will not get him or her what is wanted, and the child will gradually learn self-discipline.

3 DISTRACTION If your child's behavior is becoming difficult, involve him or her in a task and provide a running commentary on what is happening.

4 GIVE WARNINGS Tell your child that if he or she does not behave, an activity that he or she enjoys will be withdrawn.

5 AVOID PROVOKING A TANTRUM If your child is tired or over-excited, spend time with him or her. If the child has been away from home, spend a few minutes reestablishing your relationship. Be calm and reassuring.

6 GIVE POSITIVE FEEDBACK If your child has been well behaved, say so and show approval.

7 REMOVE ALL ATTENTION If you feel your child is playing to an audience, walk out of the room to show you are displeased with his or her behavior. Return after a few minutes to give reassurance.

8 SET A GOOD EXAMPLE Your child learns from you. Show that it is appropriate to express anger but not to lose control. If you show excessive anger toward your child, be prepared to apologize. Encourage your child to do the same after a tantrum.

ESSENTIAL **LIFE SKILLS**

EXPRESSING YOUR FEELINGS *See pp.88–89*

SAYING NO *See pp.90–91*

DEALING WITH ANGER *See pp.92–93*

HOW YOUR PAST AFFECTS THE PRESENT *See pp.118–119*

SELF-CARE *See pp.126–139*

ADOLESCENCE

"Every time my sister stays out late with her friends, my parents become angry, and it ends up in a fight. It is a difficult time for the whole family, but she needs space to grow up."

Know how much to let go. Between the ages of about 10 and 18, every child goes through an often difficult and self-conscious period of physical and emotional change as he or she moves from being a dependent child to being an independent adult. Adjusting to this phase, adolescence, often proves one of the greatest sources of stress for families, and an emotional time for both parents and teenagers.

PARENTS WITH ADOLESCENT CHILDREN

As a parent, you can expect to experience anger and frustration, as your child, who has always wanted to do things with you, now prefers to spend his or her time out with friends, often behaving secretively or in what appears to be a deliberately controversial way. This may lead to feelings of rejection and resentment as you interpret your child's new-found independence as exploitation of the family home for free food and lodging. Other common feelings are guilt as you question the way you have brought up your child, and jealousy of his or her apparent freedom. Your feelings are normal and natural, but you are viewing the problem solely from your own

"The only lasting things we can give our children are roots and wings."

HODDING CARTER

HOW TO COPE WITH YOUR ADOLESCENT

1 REMEMBER ADOLESCENCE IS JUST A PHASE Difficult behavior is short-term. Don't take it personally.

2 BE MORE FLEXIBLE For example, don't expect your adolescent to sit through full family meals as before.

3 RECOGNIZE YOUR OWN FEELINGS Accept feelings of frustration, and discuss your emotions with a friend or your partner.

4 PROVIDE SECURITY AND STABILITY It is important to offer a stable base for your child to return to. Support your partner's decisions and join together to present your child with a firm, united front.

5 SET RULES AND ENFORCE THEM Rules should be reasonable, realistic, and less restrictive for older children. Enforce rules by limiting access to privileges or by grounding. Be firm but fair.

6 ALLOW PRIVACY Knocking on your child's bedroom door before entering shows respect. Be prepared to install a lock if asked.

7 BE A GOOD LISTENER Listen to your child's feelings and try not to preach or overreact. Aim to boost his or her self-confidence.

8 DISCUSS ISSUES OPENLY Talk to your child frankly about smoking, drinking, drugs, and sex. Treat him or her as an equal.

point of view. To improve the situation, you need to make an attempt to understand what your child is feeling and be aware that while appearing mature in many ways, he or she still needs your love and support.

ADOLESCENTS WITH DIFFICULT PARENTS

If you are going through adolescence, this is one of the most difficult phases in your life as you develop from being a child to being an adult. You will notice rapid changes in your body, as you suddenly grow taller, get pimples, and develop pubic hair. If you are a girl, your breasts begin to develop and you start your periods, and if you are a boy your voice deepens and you have erections and ejaculations. You feel different inside and out. and it is a stressful and often embarrassing time that may make you reject your parents, who do not seem to understand.

As you adjust to the changes you are experiencing, you probably feel that you need more freedom and independence from your family. As a young adult, a new world is open to you and you may want to experiment with fashion, hairstyles, sex, and smoking or drinking. It is a time of great excitement. You feel old enough to make your own decisions and resent your parents for still treating you like a child. This is frustrating, but one way of tackling the problem is to try to view the situation from their point of view. You are changing rapidly, and it is inevitable that they are left behind. They care about you and feel responsible for you. Perhaps they also feel hurt or rejected as you become increasingly involved in your own life and do not need them as much as you did.

Educate your parents about life in your world

If your parents have not kept up with the changes in you, try to help them. Explain to them in a mature way that the rules they applied when you were a child are now less appropriate. Tell them that you need more independence and that you can achieve this only through discussion and negotiation.

NEGOTIATE WITH YOUR PARENTS

1 BE POLITE AND WILLING Saying *"please,"* speaking courteously, or doing an odd job around the house will dramatically increase your chance of getting what you want.

2 DON'T TRY TO CHANGE THE WORLD Ask for small changes at first.

3 BE HONEST ABOUT YOUR FEELINGS Discuss with your parents ways in which you irritate each other. Respect their views and be prepared to give and take.

4 WORK OUT SOLUTIONS Suggest solutions to conflicts and let your parents adopt them as their own.

5 DISCOVER WHAT THEY FEAR Push your parents to go further than saying *"You're too young."* Find out the reasons for their fears.

6 BE POSITIVE Explain how you feel rather than complaining. Expand on phrases like *"It's not fair..."* and *"I hate..."*

ESSENTIAL **LIFE SKILLS**

SIX BASIC ASSERTIVENESS SKILLS *See p.86*

DEALING WITH CRITICISM *See p.87*

EXPRESSING YOUR FEELINGS *See pp.88–89*

SAYING NO *See pp.90–91*

COMMUNICATING IN RELATIONSHIPS *See pp.116–117*

PREMENSTRUAL SYNDROME

*"I dread the two weeks before my period. My breasts are tender
and I feel unattractive. Before my period starts I usually have a headache,
I am irritable, and I feel like bursting into tears."*

"At the slightest hint of conflict I start to cry."

About 95 percent of women of reproductive age suffer some symptoms of premenstrual syndrome, or PMS, in the two weeks leading up to their monthly period. Although PMS is not, strictly speaking, a prime source of stress, many women are aware that in the few days just before a period, things often seem to "just go wrong." In addition to the physical symptoms of headaches, bloatedness, and sore breasts, you may feel tense and emotional. Those who suffer from PMS often describe symptoms as being "unable to cope" or "feeling out of control," where they behave irrationally and unreasonably. It is at this time of the month when you are most likely to drop or break things, or snap at a friend or partner, possibly causing a fight that may end in tears.

PMS is often reported as being more severe when you are already under stress, creating a vicious circle. To break the circle and regain control of your life, you need to keep a record of each menstrual schedule. By knowing the pattern you can identify your most vulnerable times and plan around them.

BE PREPARED FOR PMS

1 IDENTIFY BACKGROUND STRESSES PMS is often blamed for causing headaches and muscle pain, but some of these symptoms may be caused by underlying stresses, which you need to confront. List all the demands in your life at the moment.

2 EXPRESS YOUR EMOTIONS Talking to a close friend, a relative, or your partner can help you to relax and release tension.

3 MAKE ALLOWANCES Avoid conflict or excessive demands on yourself at vulnerable times of the month.

4 TAKE CARE OF YOURSELF Establish a regular sleeping pattern, and eat well. Cut out coffee and drink camomile tea. Evening Primrose Oil may help to relieve sore breasts. Try taking vitamin B_6, vitamin A, calcium, and magnesium.

5 REST, RELAX, AND TAKE EXERCISE Establish a regular program of relaxation and gentle exercise.

6 ACCEPT PMS AND THINK POSITIVELY Plan PMS into your life, rather than seeing it as a time when you will be unable to cope. It is a natural part of your cycle and not an illness. Accept the rhythm. Go with it, rather than fighting it.

ESSENTIAL LIFE SKILLS	EXPRESSING YOUR FEELINGS *See pp.88–89*	GOAL PLANNING *See pp.96–97*	LEARNING TO RELAX *See pp.128–129*	PHYSICAL EXERCISE *See pp.132–133*	HEALTHY EATING *See pp.134–135*

LIVING WITH PAIN

*"The pain is constantly with me. It is really wearing me down.
I can't sleep at night because of it, and I don't want to take painkillers
all the time. It's only when I am really busy that I don't notice it."*

Constant pain can wear you down, keep you from sleeping, and cause you to tighten muscles to protect the painful area. This aggravates the condition by causing tension and discomfort in other parts of your body. The constant stress eventually makes you feel preoccupied and depressed, as you see days and weeks stretch ahead with no sign of relief. Whatever the cause of your pain, however, you can learn ways of controlling it.

It is thought that there is no direct relationship between tissue damage and pain. Nerve impulses from the tissue pass through a "gate" in your spinal column, and messages from the brain, concerning how you think and feel, then act on and alter these impulses. If you are frightened, depressed, angry, or anxious, the gate opens and you will feel worse. However, if you are relaxed, happy, and active, the gate closes and your pain threshold is raised. Similarly, counter-stimulation such as heat treatment, a cold compress, or massage can effectively close the "pain gate" or take your mind off the pain.

Your state of mind can improve your tolerance of pain.

MANAGE CHRONIC PAIN

1 LEARN A RELAXATION TECHNIQUE Adopt a progressive muscle relaxation technique (*see p.129*), and breathe slowly and calmly.

2 STUDY YOUR PAIN Keep a diary of when your pain increases or decreases. Plan activities when the pain is likely to be less.

3 DISTRACT YOURSELF Fill your time with interesting activities to help distract you from the pain.

4 BE POSITIVE Write down and challenge negative thoughts such as *"This pain is getting worse,"* with positive statements such as *"I'll feel better if I relax."*

5 USE A VISUALIZATION TECHNIQUE Visualize the pain as being like the hot bars of an electric fire. Control your pain by imagining that you are "switching off" each bar one by one.

6 PACE YOURSELF Keep active, but be careful not to overdo it.

7 SET REALISTIC GOALS List your goals and reward yourself when you achieve them.

8 ASK FRIENDS FOR HELP Teach others to help you to help yourself, rather than doing things for you. Otherwise you will lose independence and have more time to focus on the pain.

ESSENTIAL LIFE SKILLS	GOAL PLANNING *See pp.96–97*	RATIONAL THINKING *See pp.104–105*	CHALLENGING DISTORTED THINKING *See pp.106–107*	LEARNING TO RELAX *See pp.128–129*	RELAXED BREATHING *See p.130*

SEPARATION AND DIVORCE

*"We have had a lot of problems over the past two years. I realize
it is no one's fault. We both have demanding careers, and with
three children to bring up we gradually stopped talking to each other."*

You can expect
to experience
feelings of loss,
similar to a
bereavement.

Separation and divorce are thought to rank second only to death of a spouse in terms of stress levels. Clearly, the two individuals directly involved suffer most, but this is a stressful time also for their families and particularly for any children. Today, in the developed world, divorce is increasingly common, affecting as many as one in three marriages. A recent survey indicated that 70 percent of divorces were instigated by women. One factor may be that many women now have a much greater level of independence and have more options available to them.

When you go through a divorce, you often experience multiple losses: a loss of a main attachment, a loss of meaning and purpose for the future, and a loss of support and companionship. You will have to cope with the legal proceedings as well as the emotional stress. However, the experience can be less painful if your feelings are better understood.

THE EMOTIONAL STAGES OF GRIEF

If you are in the early stages of separation, you should be prepared for an emotional reaction similar to that of bereavement. Your initial feeling of shock will probably be followed by protest, including such emotions as guilt, anger, and hope, then comes disorganization, where feelings of inferiority, depression, and loneliness may be prevalent. Finally, you will accept the situation and emotionally disengage yourself as you return to normal.

- GUILT If you have instigated the separation and see your former partner hurt, or he or she reminds you of the good times you once had, you may experience feelings of guilt. Giving in to these feelings and going back might well appear an ideal solution in the short term. However, unless your partner agrees to make major changes, you may be creating a long-term problem. Staying in or returning to a relationship out of pity or in continuing unhappiness is a recipe for disaster, and all the old problems are likely to reappear.

- ANGER Even if it is, at times, unpleasant, anger is a natural and useful emotion, because it serves to propel the process of separation forward and helps bring about change quickly. If anger is absent, it is possible that you either are repressing it or were never fully emotionally involved in the relationship, particularly if you are the rejected partner.

- HOPE It is said that "hope dies last," and this is certainly true for relationships. If you have been rejected and are clinging to the last straw of hope of a reconciliation after a year has passed, it might be because of the way you have parted. Has your former partner honestly explained his or her reasons for wanting to end the relationship? If the answer is "no," press your ex-partner for a straight

"If he had only told me at the time what he thought, I could have gotten on with my life."

explanation so that you can make sense of it in your own mind. If he or she has done a "disappearing act" or does not have the courage to be honest with you, then be glad he or she is gone. Your ex-partner might think that he or she is being kind by protecting you, but is only being childish and cowardly and prolonging your agony.

■ INFERIORITY If you are the rejected partner you are likely to feel hurt and may start doubting yourself. You may have distorted irrational thoughts, such as "There must be something wrong with me" or "I am a complete failure." Recognize that when people are stressed their thinking does

become distorted. Challenge these thoughts. You are not as useless as you think, and your ex-partner is not so wonderful.

■ DEPRESSION It is important to grieve, which means to go through the pain rather than avoid it. The more you can experience the pain, the sooner you will feel better.

■ LONELINESS A fear of loneliness and an inability to be alone often cause weak relationships to drag on too long. After a separation you will need to get used to spending time on your own, but it does not mean staying at home moping. Make arrangements to see friends in whom you can confide your feelings. However, beware of becoming involved in another relationship on the "rebound" or when your "neediness" may distort your feelings.

"It was hell, but my friends pulled me through."

COPING WITH SPLITTING UP

1 YOU ARE NOT THE FIRST Remind yourself that many people have suffered this pain before or are still suffering. It is a process that you will come through and be stronger for. The pain will pass.

2 EXPRESS YOUR FEELINGS Talk it through with people you are close to. Crying helps to relieve the stress and pain. Writing down your feelings can help you clarify jumbled thoughts.

3 UNDERSTAND WHAT WENT WRONG The breakdown of a relationship is as much due to your partner as you. Look for negative patterns in your relationship and understand why it has failed.

4 FILL THE EMPTINESS Make lists of jobs that need doing and get to work on them now. This is an ideal time for embarking on a new project, from clearing out the house to going on a world tour.

5 KEEP THINGS IN PERSPECTIVE Challenge negative thoughts such as *"Sam doesn't love me anymore"* with such positive statements as *"but I've got lots of friends and family who do."* Use rational thinking techniques to challenge irrational thoughts like *"I'm old and unattractive."*

6 MAKE CLEAR DECISIONS Avoid making any major decisions when you are really upset.

| ESSENTIAL LIFE SKILLS | ASSERTIVENESS *See pp.82–93* | RATIONAL THINKING *See pp.104–105* | CHALLENGING DISTORTED THINKING *See pp.106–107* | SELF-CARE *See pp.126–139* |

STEPFAMILIES

"When I remarried, I took on not only a new partner but a whole new family. I could never have anticipated what it might have been like. It is a gradual process, but we are learning to live together."

"Hearts are not had as a gift, but hearts are earned."

W. B. YEATS

Adapting to life in a new family is a stressful time for all concerned. The emotions aroused may include:

- GUILT The biological parent may feel guilt for having disrupted the child's life, the step-parent for feeling that he or she does not love the child enough, and the child for having divided loyalties between biological and stepparent.

- ANGER The child may feel angry with the stepparent for not being the natural parent.

- JEALOUSY There may be rivalry between brothers and sisters from different marriages.

It is inevitable that stepfamilies encounter more difficulties than natural families. However, if handled sensitively and with care, these new families can be successful and happy. Stepparents often achieve a feeling of satisfaction and pride from having earned the love and trust of a young person who may originally have been suspicious and resentful. Children hurt by the breakup of their parents' relationship often grow closer to the stepparent as trust develops, but it is a precarious and tricky path.

ADAPT TO NEW FAMILY MEMBERS

1 MAKE A FRESH START New accommodations can help ease problems of territoriality.

2 FACE UP TO PROBLEMS Don't pretend that everyone is happy. You are bound to have problems, and it is only by facing them that you can overcome them.

3 LET THE REAL PARENTS VISIT Allow the child time alone with the real parents if requested.

4 CARE CAN BE AS GOOD AS LOVE Show you care, but don't despair if love doesn't come. Be patient.

5 BE RATIONAL If a toddler has a tantrum or a teenager is rude, don't blame it on the fact that you are a stepfamily. These are phases that all children go through.

6 TALK AND LISTEN Mutual trust and tolerance are gained through communication and understanding.

7 TALK ABOUT YOUR ROLE Do not assume that your stepchild will view you as a parent. Rather, you may be seen as a good friend.

8 BE CAUTIOUS ABOUT DISCIPLINE Your stepchild is unlikely to accept discipline from you until you have established a good relationship, which might take a long time. Avoid head-on confrontations with adolescents.

ESSENTIAL
LIFE SKILLS

ASSERTIVENESS
See pp.82–93

RATIONAL
THINKING
See pp.104–113

IMPROVING
RELATIONSHIPS
See pp.114–115

COMMUNICATING
IN RELATIONSHIPS
See pp.116–117

EXTRAMARITAL AFFAIRS

*"I find it difficult to come to terms with the deceit. But when
I think of the children and all we have built together, I know
that we will have to find a way to rebuild our marriage."*

The effects of an affair on a long-standing relationship can be devastating, whether it is a one-night stand or a clandestine liaison that has gone on for years. The longer an affair has continued, the greater the emotional intimacy that has been allowed to build up, and the more difficult it is to go back and settle in the existing relationship.

Most people usually say that if their partner were to have an affair it would end the relationship, but in reality the majority of couples stay together. Most affairs are disasters both in themselves and in their long-term effects after they have been discovered. Affairs usually begin for a reason, probably as a result of something missing in the unfaithful partner or in the relationship itself. If you discover your partner has been unfaithful, you will probably go through a series of stages similar to the stages of grief in a bereavement. The early stages occur at the time of the immediate impact of the discovery, when you feel shock, numbness, disbelief, jealousy, and anger. The next stage contains despair and depression, culminating in a phase of reorganization and rebuilding.

However traumatic it may seem at the time, some relationships are actually strengthened by an affair, since each partner adjusts to a more positive and open relationship in which there can be no secrets.

After an affair, each partner needs to adapt to a new role.

HOW TO RECOVER FROM AN AFFAIR

1 INVESTIGATE THE CAUSES You need to discuss the underlying reasons for the affair before your relationship can move on.

2 MAKE A FRESH START An affair often ends the old relationship, and you need to rebuild it with agreed-on modifications.

3 TALK ABOUT YOUR EMOTIONS Discuss with your partner your feelings about what happened. If you cannot talk without arguing, set aside 50 minutes each week. Each partner has 25 minutes to talk while the other listens without interrupting. The affair is not discussed at other times.

4 BE PREPARED FOR CHANGE Each partner must adapt to a new role in a new relationship. The wronged partner often becomes stronger and more assertive, and the old idealistic trust is replaced by a more realistic trust, based on respect, tolerance, and the acceptance of shortcomings.

ESSENTIAL
LIFE SKILLS

ASSERTIVENESS
See pp.82–93

RATIONAL
THINKING
See pp.104–113

IMPROVING
RELATIONSHIPS
See pp.114–125

SELF-CARE
See pp.126–139

Holiday stress

"I love family gatherings and the excitement of everyone being together. But there is so much to organize. I worry that I cannot cope and will not have everything ready in time."

A holiday should be relaxing, but it can be as stressful as going to work.

Family holidays, particularly festive occasions, are supposed to be the high points of the year, but for many they can be a time of great stress and disappointment. First, there is an expectation that you will be happy and jolly, which immediately puts pressure on you. If you are feeling low, you may feel isolated and out of step with the rest of the world. Second, you alter your routines and are thrown into different situations. You may find yourself in a country where the food and climate do not suit you, or at a family party surrounded by relatives, some of whom you do not get along with. Third, holidays are times of great decision-making and planning as you work out where to go, who to invite, what to eat, and how much money to spend.

One way of enjoying your holiday is to avoid unrealistic expectations of the kind often portrayed by the media. The reality is more likely to be children arguing and petty squabbles between adults. It is fine to look forward to time off from work, but do not expect bliss, then you will not be too disappointed if it falls short.

Be ready for the holidays

1 **Prepare for parties** Plan first and then relax. Make difficult decisions early on, pace yourself, and make lists so that you know what you need to do and when.

2 **Share responsibility** Don't be a martyr. Much preparation can be shared. Delegate tasks and ask for help. Communicate openly and say no. If you carry all the burden, resentment may build up.

3 **Keep your personal space** Carve out some time, space, and solitude amid the change of routine and the social frenzy. Plan your time so that you can be alone to recharge your batteries, even if for only a short time.

4 **Express your true feelings** If you are feeling down or left out, express your feelings to someone close or write them down.

5 **Do not overspend** Set a budget and keep to it. Some people prefer to open a separate holiday account.

6 **Challenge worrying thoughts** 'If you find yourself worrying, *"There is too much to do, I'll never be ready in time,"* challenge that thought with *"Calm down. One step at a time. I'll be fine."*

ESSENTIAL LIFE SKILLS	ASSERTIVENESS *See pp.82–93*	GOAL PLANNING *See pp.96–97*	DELEGATION *See pp.100–101*	CHALLENGING DISTORTED THINKING *See pp.106–107*	SELF-CARE *See pp.126–139*

MIDLIFE CRISIS

"Where did my life go? I can't believe I am 45 already, and what do I have to show for it? My life has hardly changed over the last 15 years, and I can't see it improving between now and when I retire."

By the time you get to your forties, you have probably reached the midpoint of your life. For the first time, you may start to notice real signs of aging, such as gray hairs, weight gain, and wrinkles. You may also find that emotionally this is a time of stress as you take stock of your current situation and ask yourself, "What have I achieved?" "What is there to look forward to?" and "Am I happy with my life?" Your forties can also be a stressful time when major life events are likely to occur, such as parents dying and children leaving home. After years of striving to make it to the top, your career ambitions may also reach a plateau, and it is common for boredom

or disenchantment to set in. You might think, "I do not want to do this for the rest of my life." This can also be a time when you scrutinize your relationship and find it wanting.

"Suddenly I feel time is running out."

During your forties, you may enter into a period of crisis, which is a sort of desperation to do things before you are too old. This happens particularly with people who married young and missed the chance to experiment with different relationships. Similarly, people who have done the same job for years may feel a need to experience something new.

HOW TO SURVIVE YOUR MIDLIFE CRISIS

1 PURSUE YOUR INTERESTS
If, until now, you have invested a lot of effort in establishing yourself at work and within your family, now might be the time to start to think about yourself and ways in which you can develop your "shadow side." You may want to exploit your full potential and invest time in a new hobby, a musical instrument, a creative activity,

or a sport, or enroll in a college or an evening course. You may find that you do not need to make dramatic changes, but can add a new dimension to your life by introducing a new element.

2 PLAN YOUR FUTURE It may help to take time out and write a list of all the things you would like to achieve with the second half of your life. Instead of

imagining your future as bleak, visualize it as a time full of opportunities and possibilities.

3 BECOME INVOLVED Boost your self-esteem and give yourself a sense of belonging by taking up charity work, joining a club, or becoming involved in local politics, where you are able to help others and meet new people.

ESSENTIAL
LIFE SKILLS

GOAL
PLANNING
See pp.96–97

OVERCOMING
PROCRASTINATION
See p.98

DEVELOPING HOBBIES
AND INTERESTS
See p.136

EXPANDING YOUR
CIRCLE OF FRIENDS
See p.137

BEREAVEMENT AND LOSS

*"It is difficult to come to terms with the feelings of devastation
and total loss. Some days I don't feel too bad,
but other days I feel I cannot go on."*

You cannot
hurry the
period of
grieving

Bereavement means "the loss of something valued." Grieving is a process of adjusting to that loss and is universally recognized across all cultures. The process of grieving usually occurs when the loss involves a death, but it can also be applied to other situations, including the breakup of a relationship or divorce, loss of a job, or coming to terms with loss of health through an illness or a disability. Research into comparative levels of stress connected with important life events (*see pp.44–45*) shows that the death of a spouse is regarded as the most stressful event. Grieving is more difficult if the death is sudden or violent, or if the relationship was very close or one in which one or both partners were very dependent. When you experience a serious loss of

someone close, you can experience the following four recognized stages of grief, each of which is accompanied by a range of different emotions:

- STAGE ONE: SHOCK The reality of the loss often takes time to sink in. Your initial reactions may vary from numbness, denial, disbelief, and hysteria, to not being able to think straight. These are all natural emotions that cushion you against the loss and allow you to experience it more slowly and cope with it better in the short term.

- STAGE TWO: PROTEST At this stage, it is normal to protest that the loss cannot be real, even though you are being confronted with evidence that it is. As you struggle between denying and eventually accepting the reality of what has happened, you experience waves of strong and powerful feelings, such as anger, guilt, sadness, fear, yearning, and searching.

THE GRIEF WHEEL

When you lose someone close to you, it is natural to experience a wide range of emotions that correspond with a number of recognized stages of grief. The emotions you feel vary from person to person, and you will not always move through these stages in a logical progression. Some people might experience them in rapid succession; others more haphazardly over a period of months.

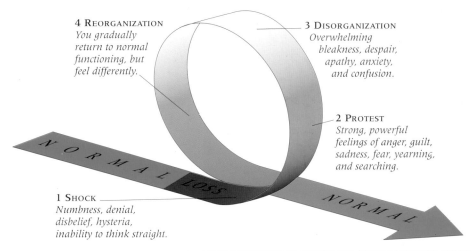

4 REORGANIZATION
You gradually return to normal functioning, but feel differently.

3 DISORGANIZATION
Overwhelming bleakness, despair, apathy, anxiety, and confusion.

2 PROTEST
Strong, powerful feelings of anger, guilt, sadness, fear, yearning, and searching.

1 SHOCK
Numbness, denial, disbelief, hysteria, inability to think straight.

NORMAL LOSS NORMAL

■ STAGE THREE: DISORGANIZATION This is the stage when the reality of the loss is only too real. You are likely to experience overwhelming feelings of bleakness, despair, apathy, anxiety, and confusion. You may feel that this depression could go on forever and that there is no way out.

■ STAGE FOUR: REORGANIZATION You begin to rebuild your life and acquire a greater balance. At last you are able to choose to remember happier times. Gradually you return to previous functioning, but often with changed values and new meaning in life.

FACE THE PAIN

Grieving, though painful, is a natural process that must be acknowledged and worked through. Some people will wrongly try to avoid that pain by keeping themselves very busy or burying themselves in work. Other people might defend themselves against the pain by saying to themselves, "I have to be strong for everybody else" or "It's no use crying." The period of grieving cannot be hurried and may vary from days to weeks, months, or even years. Even when you feel you are over it, you must be prepared for occasional setbacks, perhaps when you hear a particular piece of music, smell a certain scent, or remember a shared anniversary.

It is understandable to want to spend time alone, but it does not help to become too isolated. Talking and listening are important throughout all stages of grief, but it is quite usual for friends and acquaintances to feel embarrassed and not know what to say. When you are ready, approach your friends and say, "I need to talk" or "I need some practical help." There will be days when you prefer not to talk about it. When this happens, it is best just to be honest and explain your feelings to other people.

COME TO TERMS WITH YOUR GRIEF

1 ACCEPT THE LOSS It is natural to protect yourself from the full impact of the loss by holding on to the deceased's belongings. Although it may take time, being able to release those possessions is a positive sign of acceptance and reorganization.

2 FEEL THE PAIN Recognize and experience your emotions. Crying helps, since it allows painful feelings to be expressed.

3 TALK ABOUT IT Talking about the loss and reminiscing helps you to accept the situation. Expressing regrets, fears, and anger is helpful. Do not take the attitude that *"it doesn't help to rake it up."*

4 TAKE ONE DAY AT A TIME Do not try to sort out everything at once. Grieving takes as long as it takes – there are no fixed time limits and it cannot be hurried.

5 TAKE CARE OF YOURSELF Get plenty of rest, eat well, take time to retreat, and time to talk. Try not to become isolated but seek out social support.

6 ADAPT TO CHANGE This may mean taking on a new role, learning new skills, or learning how to live on your own.

7 LET GO When you are ready, let go. This does not mean forget.

ESSENTIAL LIFE SKILLS	EXPRESSING YOUR FEELINGS *See pp.88–89*	DEALING WITH ANGER *See pp.92–93*	RATIONAL THINKING *See pp.104–105*	COMMUNICATING IN RELATIONSHIPS *See pp.116–117*	SELF-CARE *See pp.126–139*

ACCIDENTS AND TRAUMA

"I can't forget it – images keep flashing through my mind and I have difficulty sleeping. I am trying to return to my normal life, but at the moment everything seems remote and unreal."

"Why did it have to happen to me?"

Accidents happen all the time, but in most cases you deal with them quickly and then get on with your life. However, if something happens that is serious enough to undermine one or more of your fundamental beliefs, this experience can be described as trauma, and the effects will be a lot more difficult to come to terms with. The greater the contradiction between what has happened and the belief, the more likely the trauma. If you strongly believe, for example, that the world is an orderly, predictable, and safe place, that life is meaningful, or that you are a strong and competent person, and this belief is challenged by a catastrophic event, then traumatic stress is most likely to ensue.

Trauma "pierces or wounds your body's psychological defenses." You might say, "It has upset me, it really got through to me." Events that create trauma might range from being involved in or witnessing an armed robbery, a traffic accident, or an assault, to experiencing physical or sexual abuse, a fire, a plane or train crash, war, or another disaster. You do not have to be directly involved to suffer trauma. When the ferry the *Herald of Free Enterprise* sank off the Belgian coast in 1986, with great loss of life, it was estimated that out of a total of 10,000 people traumatized, at least four out of five were rescue workers or relatives and friends of the victims.

PHYSICAL EFFECTS OF TRAUMA

If you have had a traumatic experience, as well as the huge range of emotions you are having to try to deal with – such as fear, guilt, shame, or anger – it is quite normal to feel tired and have low energy levels. You may be tearful and unable to concentrate or remember events correctly. You might feel cut off or disinterested, irritable, and intolerant of others, and you may suffer pains and headaches due to increased tension in your muscles. Many people complain of feeling in a state of arousal, unable to sleep correctly and troubled by nightmares

---

NORMAL EMOTIONS ASSOCIATED WITH TRAUMA

- FEAR This may be fear of it happening again, of breaking down, of being alone, of damage to yourself and loved ones.

- GUILT You may feel guilty for surviving or for being better off than others.

- REGRETS You may regret things not done.

- SHAME You may feel ashamed for not having acted as you would have wished, or for having been seen as emotional.

- ANGER It is usual to feel anger for what happened, at who caused it, or at other people's seeming lack of understanding.

- DISAPPOINTMENT You may feel disappointed for all the plans you never fulfilled, which are now impossible.

---

and flashbacks. Be aware that severe trauma can also turn relationships sour. You may feel that you have so much to cope with that you cannot give as much to your partner or family as before. You may even feel that you have changed, and that they do not understand you.

RETURNING TO NORMAL

After a traumatic experience, it is most important to get back to normal as soon as possible. Try to express your emotions and don't bottle up your feelings. Go over the experience again and again, both on your own and by talking about it with friends. Try to keep to your normal routine. Go to work, do the shopping, and keep your children at school even if they have been traumatized, too. Do not forget that children experience similar feelings, so talk with them and let them express themselves. The essential thing is to try not to avoid situations or triggers that bring back painful memories of the event; this will delay emotional sequencing.

This is a very stressful time, and it is important that you take care of yourself. Make sure that you eat well, allow time to relax, and get plenty of rest. Be extra careful in the car and at home, since accidents are more common after severe stress. Don't expect the memories to go – they will gradually soften, but the feelings will stay with you for a long time and you need to learn to live with them.

If after a few months you are still suffering persistent symptoms of anxiety, flashbacks, dreams, and intrusive thoughts, and you find you are avoiding anything that might be linked with the event, you are probably suffering Post-Traumatic Stress Disorder, or PTSD, and should seek professional help.

Although individuals may be adversely affected by catastrophe, many report that once they overcome the initial intense feelings they can feel strengthened. After the *Herald of Free Enterprise* disaster, 35 percent of those interviewed felt that they had ultimately been affected positively.

HOW TO RECOVER FROM TRAUMA

1 ACCEPT FEELINGS OF NUMBNESS Your mind allows the misfortune to be felt little by little.

2 KEEP ACTIVE You might find that helping others gives you some relief. However, be careful not to undertake too many responsibilities. Overactivity is often detrimental if it is a way of blocking memories of the event.

3 SEEK SUPPORT Discuss your feelings with close friends and family, and allow them to offer you physical and emotional support.

4 PUT ASIDE TIME FOR PRIVACY To process your feelings, you will find it necessary, at times, to be alone or just with family and close friends.

5 CONFRONT THE REALITY Be careful not to avoid memories of the event. Attend funerals and return to the scene of the event.

6 PROCESS YOUR FEELINGS It helps to think, talk, and dream about the event. The more you can do this, the better the emotional processing and the quicker you can continue with your life.

| ESSENTIAL LIFE SKILLS | EXPRESSING YOUR FEELINGS See pp.88–89 | DEALING WITH ANGER See pp.92–93 | RATIONAL THINKING See pp.104–105 | CHALLENGING DISTORTED THINKING See pp.106–107 | SELF-CARE See pp.126–139 |

EXAM STRESS

"As the day of the exam draws closer, I feel more and more agitated, even when I know I am well prepared. I am so terrified that my mind will go blank. I sometimes feel physically sick."

Exams are a game. Know the rules.

Studying for and taking exams are acquired skills, or techniques. The skill of "how to study" is rarely taught at school, although a great deal of attention is given to the content of study. Exam nerves, worry, or fear of failure are normal for even the most talented student. Use this energy to motivate yourself. If your mind strays into negative thinking, recognize that your thoughts have become exaggerated and distorted. You are probably making "catastrophic," "all or nothing" predictions that need to be challenged or ignored.

It helps if your working environment is pleasant and neat. Try to limit your study to short periods with regular breaks. Research shows that after 40–50 minutes, most people's concentration diminishes, so do not study for blocks of more than 90 minutes. Treat yourself at the end of each study period, perhaps to a cup of tea and a cookie.

Be selective in your preexamination reading. You cannot hope to read whole academic tomes, so pick out relevant sections and take brief notes. Above all, approach an exam as a "game" that you want to win. Have a strategy and concentrate on keeping calm.

PREPARE YOURSELF FOR EXAMS

1 TAKE AN OVERVIEW Weigh your strengths and weaknesses, and decide what you need to know. Look at old examination papers and predict the area you need to study.

2 PLAN A REVISION TIMETABLE Work out which subjects to study each day and for how long. Allow some downtime and take one day a week off. Pin your timetable on the wall and keep to it.

3 CONDENSE YOUR NOTES Make notes on large pieces of paper using numbered points and color. Boil these down to numbered key ideas written on an index card, which you can glance at before the exam.

4 SPACE OUT REVISION PERIODS You learn more if you space your revision over longer intervals. After you have studied your notes, review them, then look at

them the next day, then perhaps two days later. Increase the length of time between revision periods but decrease the amount of time spent on each one.

5 ON THE EXAMINATION DAY Concentrate on staying calm. It is too late to learn new material, so focus on condensed notes. Read the question carefully, then plan your answer for a few minutes before beginning.

ESSENTIAL LIFE SKILLS

| MANAGING YOUR TIME *See pp.94–103* | RATIONAL THINKING *See pp.104–105* | CHALLENGING DISTORTED THINKING *See pp.106–107* | DEMOLISH YOUR WORRIES *See pp.112–113* | LEARNING TO RELAX *See pp.128–129* |

FINANCIAL DIFFICULTIES

"Lack of money is a constant worry at home and the source of most of our arguments. Living within a strict budget is difficult, and we are having to forego luxuries such as family outings, new clothes, and vacations."

Money worries can create enormous stress, particularly when they threaten the way you live, your home, and your family. A lack of money, whether it is chronic or sudden, can cause great tension and arguments between family members. Financial difficulties can be created by events beyond your control such as job loss, overspending, or low income.

If you are experiencing money problems, you need to analyze your views on financial planning and find a way of managing your finances. You cannot leave your money to look after itself or abdicate responsibility for looking after it to others.

Good money management involves being clear about what you want from life, making realistic plans to make sure it happens, and then taking control of your finances.

If you find yourself in debt, there are a number of steps you can take. Work out the extent of the debt and then how much money you have left each month after paying for essentials. Discuss the problem with your family and agree to go on an economy drive. If you have a mortgage, talk to your lender and discuss suspending payments for a period. Do not panic. Few people go bankrupt compared with the many who learn to avoid it.

MANAGE YOUR MONEY

1 KEEP TRACK Keep a written summary of all your finances. Itemize money in your checking and savings accounts, and note major bills to be paid. Every month study this piece of paper and record changes.

2 HAVE A SYSTEM Keep organized records of all your bills and financial documents in a safe place, such as a portable filing system.

3 BALANCE YOUR INVESTMENTS Don't "put all your eggs in one basket." A good rule is to put one-third of your capital in property, one-third in a safe investment, and one-third in a slightly riskier option.

4 PLAN AHEAD Try to start each year no worse off and hopefully better off than the previous one. Balance income and expenditure. Don't be overambitious.

5 KEEP AN EMERGENCY FUND Put aside a reasonable sum to enable you to cope with emergencies.

6 PAY OFF CREDIT CARDS Don't be taken in by special financial deals – nothing is free.

7 ASK QUESTIONS Before parting with your money, ask about hidden costs and if you can change your mind. If in doubt, don't sign.

ESSENTIAL LIFE SKILLS	SAYING NO *See pp.90–91*	GOAL PLANNING *See pp.96–97*	RATIONAL THINKING *See pp.104–105*	HOW TO THINK LESS RIGIDLY *See p.109*	DEMOLISH YOUR WORRIES *See pp.112–113*

CARING FOR THE ELDERLY

"He has been getting worse for two years now. He's confused and forgetful. It's hard work, because not only do I have to look after him, but I've lost his friendship and support."

Before you can care for someone else, you need to take care of yourself.

In modern developed society, improved medical care and higher standards of living have dramatically increased life expectancy. It is estimated that 20 percent of the population are of retirement age. Of these, only 6 percent are in institutions while others are often looked after in the community by a network of caregivers, many of whom are unpaid family members.

Deciding how to take care of a close relative who is elderly and whose mental functioning is deteriorating, can cause many practical problems, as well as triggering a wide range of emotions. Once it has been ascertained that he or she can no longer manage alone, you are faced with a number of options, which you should talk through with the elderly person before making any decisions.

Work out the comparative advantages and disadvantages of moving your relative into a good residential home, perhaps moving him or her into smaller accommodation near to you so that you can visit regularly, or moving your relative into your home. This last option is likely to have a domino effect on all the relationships in your house. It may also be time to make arrangements regarding financial affairs and so legal advice may be in order.

Before you can effectively help or care for an elderly relative, you must be able to look after yourself. Recognize the need to be assertive and work on developing good self-care skills. You need to eat well and take exercise, maintain your own friends and interests, arrange time off to be alone with your family, and take breaks and vacations. Beware of feeling guilty about not doing enough. You will never be able to make everything right. Often, it is a question of making the best of a bad situation.

As you watch your relative's condition deteriorate, you may have to cope with a wide range of feelings. A role reversal takes place as you care for your parent in ways that he or she cared for you as a small child. For example, you may need to take your parent to the bathroom. If he or she becomes incontinent, tell your

DO YOU TAKE CARE OF YOURSELF?

In order to help others and offer them your support, you need to take care of yourself. How well do you do this? Answer the following questions and find out.

- Do you still go on vacation?

- Do you go out socially once a week?

- Do you have someone you can talk to?

- Do you have any practical help?

- Is there anyone to stand in for you?

doctor and, if there is no medical cause, ask to be referred to a continence adviser. You can help avoid nighttime bedwetting in the short term by gradually reducing quantities of fluid throughout the day.

COPING WITH CONFUSION

If your relative becomes ill, dependent, or confused, you may feel you have lost a companion and an important relationship. In many ways, the person you knew and loved has gone, and you must grieve the loss, experiencing feelings associated with bereavement, while he or she is still there in person. It is common also to feel guilty, particularly if you lose your temper, feel embarrassed at odd behavior, or wish that he or she were not there. Do not expect yourself to be perfect. If your relative is confused, make sure he or she is in comforting, familiar surroundings. Establishing a regular daily routine will help reduce confusion. Talk slowly, allowing enough time for a response. If he or she is having difficulty communicating, try to guess the meaning or feeling behind the words rather than taking every word literally. If your relative's short-term memory is impaired, his or her long-term memory is probably still intact. Feel free to reminisce about past events, since this may well be your richest area of communication. It helps to have a sense of humor, so try to laugh with the elderly person at the situations you both find yourself in. Look for the moments that bring pleasure and closeness. Holding hands, touching, and talking intimately can often cut through the confusion.

A sense of humor and the ability to laugh will help you to cope.

HOW TO CARE FOR AN ELDERLY PERSON

1 ALLOW FOR CHANGE However much it upsets you to see a relative eat with a spoon rather than a knife and fork, or use a toilet chair rather than the toilet, do your best to accept this change rather than fight it.

2 ENCOURAGE INDEPENDENCE The longer people can do things for themselves, the more they retain their dignity. Offer help, but try not to take over.

3 SHARE THE RESPONSIBILITY Resentment can build up if you feel that other members of your family are not pulling their weight. You must ask for help assertively and say that you need a break.

4 PROTECT YOUR OWN INTERESTS Maintain an interest or a hobby outside the home to distract you from your daily routine. Stay in contact with your friends.

5 TAKE BREAKS It is essential for both you and the person you are caring for to have breaks from each other. You need to make sure you take regular days off as well as at least two weeks' vacation a year. Plan your time off and make arrangements for someone else to fill in for you.

6 TALK TO SOMEONE CLOSE Try not to bottle up your feelings, but air them with somebody close.

| ESSENTIAL LIFE SKILLS | ASSERTIVENESS *See pp.82–93* | CONTROLLING PERFECTIONISM *See p 99* | DELEGATION *See pp.100–101* | HOW TO THINK LESS RIGIDLY *See p.109* | SELF-CARE *See pp.126–139* |

PUBLIC SPEAKING

"I always become very anxious before speaking in public. However, if I prepare thoroughly and rehearse what I am going to say, I usually manage quite well."

For many people, speaking in front of an audience can be a terrifying experience, causing symptoms of acute stress such as sweating, rapid heartbeat, and panic. Whether it is a job interview, a speech at a wedding, or a speech to a conference of hundreds of people, the techniques are the same. Speaking in public seldom comes naturally, and most people have to learn how to do it. Although most of us will never become charismatic orators, we can learn to be competent and turn the adrenalin into positive energy.

One way of overcoming your fear of speaking in public is to prepare in advance. Write down the body of your speech in full and then summarize the main points and key ideas on index cards. The three oldest rules for making a speech are "Tell them what you are going to tell them, tell them, and then tell them what you have told them." Keep the content simple and original – and remember, audiences prefer personal anecdotes.

Confidence comes with preparation

TEN TIPS FOR SPEAKING IN PUBLIC

1 REHEARSE YOUR SPEECH
Practice your speech aloud in front of a friend or a mirror. Go through from beginning to end, without pausing. Time yourself.

2 USE SMALL INDEX CARDS
Write out your speech and highlight headings and key words. Deliver the ideas in your own words, rather than reading.

3 CHECK THE SETTING BEFOREHAND
Make sure the microphone or overhead projector is in the right place. Do you have all you need?

4 RESEARCH YOUR AUDIENCE
Find out what they know about the topic. What are their interests?

5 EXERCISE EARLY IN THE DAY
This stimulates the production of endorphines, which calm nerves.

6 AVOID CAFFEINE BEFOREHAND
Caffeine can exaggerate stress responses, particularly shaking.

7 WEAR LIGHT CLOTHING
Lightweight clothing is more comfortable if you perspire.

8 TRY A BREATHING EXERCISE
Focus on one spot, place your fingers on your stomach, and breathe slowly from your abdomen *(see p.130)*.

9 HAVE A GLASS OF WATER HANDY
Make sure you have something to sip in case your mouth gets dry.

10 PAUSE BEFORE BEGINNING
On the podium take a couple of slow breaths, then slowly greet the audience. Speak slowly. If your heart is racing, ignore it. Nobody can see it.

| ESSENTIAL LIFE SKILLS | CHALLENGING DISTORTED THINKING *See pp.106–107* | LADDERING YOUR THOUGHTS *See p.110* | POSITIVE SELF-STATEMENTS *See p.111* | LEARNING TO RELAX *See pp.128–129* | RELAXED BREATHING *See p.130* |

WORK STRESS

*"I have more to do than anyone else, I can't possibly
do everything during the day. I often end up
taking work home with me"*

Work stress is the single most important cause of stress throughout the developed world. In a recent study of financial institutions, 64 percent of employers regarded excessive stress as the principal health threat facing the company.

With the introduction of new high-speed information technology, increased global competitiveness, and reduced staff levels, employees have less job security. They are carrying heavier workloads and working longer hours in an attempt to keep their jobs. A marked increase in stress levels at work is being experienced on a universal scale. There are two ways of tackling work stress:

▪ Identify sources of stress in your job and try to make appropriate changes. People often blame themselves for their problems at work rather than questioning the job itself.

▪ Examine your strategies for coping with work stress (*see pp.74–75*) and see whether these can be improved. When you are stressed, you may adopt unhelpful short-term strategies, such as missing lunch, taking work home, putting off tasks, working too late, or drinking too much. In the long term, these ways of coping usually cause difficulties.

Identify
the sources
of stress in
your job.

TWELVE WAYS OF COPING WITH WORK STRESS

1 EXPRESS YOUR FEELINGS Don't bottle up feelings and emotions.

2 MAKE TIME FOR SOCIAL ACTIVITIES Don't squeeze out hobbies, leisure, or outings with friends.

3 DON'T PUT THINGS OFF Do tasks now and don't avoid them.

4 DELEGATE Don't try to do everything yourself.

5 LEARN TO SAY NO Don't agree to take on too much.

6 PLAN REGULAR BREAKS Stop for coffee, lunch, and evenings, as well as weekends and vacations.

7 DON'T WORK TOO LONG HOURS

8 DON'T BECOME ADDICTED Try not to become reliant on alcohol, cigarettes, drugs, or food.

9 SEPARATE WORK FROM HOME Don't regularly take work home.

10 DON'T BE A PERFECTIONIST You can't get things perfect every time. Aim for 80 percent.

11 SEEK SUPPORT Openly discuss difficulties and ask for help.

12 KEEP A PERSPECTIVE It is only a job – not your life.

ESSENTIAL LIFE SKILLS	ASSERTIVENESS *See pp.82–93*	MANAGING YOUR TIME *See pp.94–103*	RATIONAL THINKING *See pp.104–113*	SELF-CARE *See pp.126–139*

IDENTIFY SOURCES OF WORK STRESS

If you can identify the causes of your stress at work you may be able to develop skills to counteract it. For each situation described below, decide how much stress it is creating for you.

SCORING
High stress 3 • Moderate stress 2 • Low stress 1 • No stress 0

1 Too much work to do

2 Too many different roles to play

3 Being responsible for managing others

4 My relationship with others at work

5 My wages/salary

6 Continuing to work at home

7 Working long or unsociable hours

8 Unclear about what is expected of me

9 Having to make decisions or plans

10 My relationship with my manager

11 Doing a job that does not challenge me

12 Difficulty switching off at home

13 Too many demands on my time

14 Having few clear objectives

15 Dealing with conflict

16 Little encouragement and support

17 Career and promotion prospects

18 The demands of work on my home life

19 Too little work to do

20 Changes in the way I'm asked to work

21 Work politics

22 Lack of colleagues to confide in

23 An unpleasant physical environment

24 Prioritizing between work and home

25 Time pressures and deadlines

26 Lack of variety and stimulation

27 Fear of making a mistake

28 Poor training and guidelines

29 Lack of job satisfaction

30 My partner's attitude toward my work

31 Not having the right skills for the job

32 Little feedback about my performance

33 Meetings/giving presentations

34 The general morale of the workplace

35 Job insecurity or threat of layoffs

36 Changes outside work – finance, illness

INTERPRETING YOUR SCORE

Transfer your scores for individual questions across the following columns of boxes. Each column will show how you score in particular areas of your work. Add up the scores in each column to find out the areas on which you need to concentrate most.

A		B		C		D		E		F	
1		2		3		4		5		6	
7		8		9		10		11		12	
13		14		15		16		17		18	
19		20		21		22		23		24	
25		26		27		28		29		30	
31		32		33		34		35		36	
TOTAL		TOTAL		TOTAL		TOTAL		TOTAL		TOTAL	

A: Workload

Over 8 Your workload appears to be creating stress. Seek to make changes in the structure of your job.

5–8 Your workload is on the verge of being stressful.

Below 5 Overload may not be an issue, but a high score for question 19 may indicate that underload is a problem.

See ASSERTIVENESS *pp.82–93*
MANAGING YOUR TIME *pp.94–103.*

B: Role

Over 8 Your job description appears to need clarifying and defining. Confront your manager assertively and make changes.

5–8 Some clarification is needed regarding your role at work.

Below 5 Your role at work does not appear to be a problem.

See ASSERTIVENESS *pp.82–93*
MANAGING YOUR TIME *pp.94–103.*

C: Responsibility

Over 8 You appear to be uncomfortable with your present responsibilities. You may benefit from talking to colleagues who have more experience of responsibility. Ask for more training.

5–8 You seem to have difficulties taking responsibility at work.

Below 5 You do not appear to have a problem with responsibility.

See ASSERTIVENESS *pp.82–93*
RATIONAL THINKING *pp.104–113.*

D: Relationships

Over 8 Relationships at work appear to be creating stress. Aim to improve the quality of these and seek better support from those around you.

5–8 Your relationships at work could be a source of stress.

Below 5 Relationships at work do not appear to be a problem.

See ASSERTIVENESS *pp.82–93*
IMPROVING RELATIONSHIPS *pp.114–125.*

E: Job satisfaction

Over 8 You appear to have a low level of job satisfaction and possibly do not feel valued at work. Are you doing the right job? Are there more satisfying areas that you could move into?

5–8 Your job could be more satisfying.

Below 5 You appear to enjoy your work.

See ASSERTIVENESS *pp.82–93*
MANAGING YOUR TIME *pp.94–103*
SELF-CARE *pp.126–139.*

F: Home/work interface

Over 8 You seem not to be keeping home and work separate. You may need to reestablish those firm boundaries.

5–8 Home and work show signs of interacting negatively.

Below 5 The interaction between home and work does not appear to be stressful.

See MANAGING YOUR TIME *pp.94–103*
SELF-CARE *pp.126–139.*

LIFE WITHOUT WORK

"I lost my job after twenty years with the same company.
It's a struggle to keep up my morale and not become too negative.
My confidence has taken a blow and my marriage has suffered."

"Preserve order amid change... and change amid order."

A.N. WHITEHEAD

Having no work, through unemployment or retirement, comes high on the list of stressful life events (*see pp.44–45*) and can cause symptoms of stress such as raised blood pressure, low self-esteem, and depression. You are forced to spend more time at home, which, if you have a family, can put a strain on relationships as you all adapt to new roles. In some ways, loss of work is like a bereavement, since you experience many losses including income, status, social contact, routine, purpose and direction, and sense of achievement.

If your job loss is sudden or unexpected, as with a bereavement, there is a gradual process of adjustment, involving shock, denial, anger, disorganization, depression, and then reorganization and eventual acceptance. Husbands may have to adjust to a change of role, with their wives becoming the main breadwinner, making them feel vulnerable and inadequate. If you have been used to getting up and going to work each morning, to be suddenly told that you are no longer required can have a devastating emotional effect. You may feel rejected and useless. You ask yourself, "What hope have I got now? I'll never be able to find another job." Of course these are negative thoughts, and it is important to challenge them with positive

COPING WITH UNEMPLOYMENT

1 MAKE FINDING A JOB YOUR JOB
Being unemployed has some similarities with being self-employed insofar as your whole day is your own. Nobody is going to tell you what to do or give you orders. Try to view the situation as a personal challenge, a new job to take on board.

2 PLAN YOUR TIME Accept that you are going to be unemployed for at least two months and plan how you are going to use that

time. This strategy reduces some of the uncertainty. Plan each day and each week, having a daily list of things to do, even if it is something simple like visiting the library to read the paper.

3 STAY ACTIVE AND FEEL POSITIVE
• Use this time as an opportunity to learn new skills. Enroll on a course or evening class.
• Try to keep yourself physically fit by getting exercise such as walking, swimming, or running.

• Take care of your appearance – if you look well groomed you will feel more confident.
• Visit places of interest.
• Treat yourself, particularly if you are feeling low. Go for a walk and buy yourself something small, even if it is only a favorite magazine.

4 LOOK ON THE BRIGHT SIDE
Remember that this temporary crisis could be a chance for self-exploration and a new direction.

Making a list of your assets boosts confidence.

rational thoughts. Tell yourself that "there is no such thing as a job for life these days," or "I am a good worker. Someone is sure to want to employ me." It is important to realize, however, that finding a new job may take time. If you can be flexible, be prepared to move to where the work is. See your situation positively, and view this as an opportunity to change direction. Explore the possibility of further education, and use the time to work out what you really want to do.

To find a job, you need to be able to sell yourself, which means you need to be aware of your own strengths. Make a list of your assets, using the following categories:

• KNOWLEDGE. What subjects do you know about? What could you talk about at length if somebody asked you to? Think broadly; this does not need to be work-related.

• EXPERIENCE Make a note of experience you have gained either in or or out of work.

• SKILLS Do you have special skills? These do not need to be work-related and may include anything from good communication skills to expertise in a sport, such as sailing.

• ABILITIES AND APTITUDE Where do your natural abilities lie? Are you a practical person or do you prefer intellectual activities?

RETIREMENT

Retiring after a lifetime of hard work can be a stressful time. If your work has been the main focus of your life, you are likely to find it difficult to fill your empty days, and depression and boredom may set in. However, unlike sudden unemployment, you have the advantage of time to plan for your retirement. Bearing in mind that retirement is usually easier for people who have interests and an active social life outside of work, make time during your last few years in employment to start widening your interests, so retirement will not come as a sudden shock. Remember, the key to a happy, healthy retirement is good planning and keeping busy.

PLAN FOR YOUR RETIREMENT

1 PREPARE IN ADVANCE
Try to anticipate problems. Are you prepared financially? If you are worried about having no work at all, you could consider taking a part-time job or getting involved in charity or voluntary work. Reevaluate your goals in life.

2 MAKE THE MOST OF FREEDOM
Retirement gives you the chance to do all the things you have always wanted. Try to see it as a new beginning. You might decide to study, learn a new skill, travel, meet new people, or take up a new sport or hobby.

3 CHALLENGE YOUR FEARS
If you have thoughts like *"I have nothing more to contribute,"* challenge them with *"I am only 65, I could have another 20 years' of active life ahead of me."* These negative thoughts are typical of distorted "all or nothing" thinking.

ESSENTIAL LIFE SKILLS	ASSERTIVENESS *See pp.82–93*	GOAL PLANNING *See pp.96–97*	RATIONAL THINKING *See pp.104–113*	PHYSICAL EXERCISE *See pp.132–133*	DEVELOPING HOBBIES AND INTERESTS *See p.136*

LIFE SKILLS

ASSERTIVENESS

MANAGING YOUR TIME

RATIONAL THINKING

IMPROVING RELATIONSHIPS

SELF-CARE

HOW WELL DO YOU COPE?

This questionnaire assesses the effectiveness of your "life skills,"
or your way of coping with stress. Read each of the statements, and decide
which score best describes how you behave at present.

SCORING
Always 4 • Often 3 • Sometimes 2 • Rarely 1 • Never 0

1 I can ask for help from others.

2 I manage my time so I am not rushed.

3 When I am upset or depressed I can figure out what thoughts lie behind it.

4 I discuss my worries with friends.

5 I make a point of looking after myself in terms of diet, health, and appearance.

6 I put off doing difficult things and avoid difficult situations.

7 I express emotions openly and directly.

8 I work toward my own personal goals.

9 I accept situations that I cannot change.

10 I can trust my partner, share feelings with, and talk frankly to him/her.

11 I reward myself with something pleasant when I've done a good job.

12 I tend to bottle up my emotions and withdraw from people.

13 I can say no to the demands of others and refuse requests.

14 I am careful how much I take on and balance this against my limited time.

15 I weigh both sides of an argument.

16 I feel close to and talk openly with members of my family.

17 I make time for my hobbies and leisure.

18 When I'm under pressure the pleasant, relaxing activities get squeezed out.

19 I complain in a store if service is poor.

20 I delegate tasks to others if I need to.

21 I can usually relate my upset mood to a specific event that has happened to me.

22 I socialize with friends.

23 I believe I need to be selfish at times.

24 I tend to avoid challenging situations.

25 I like to share my ideas with others even if they don't agree.

26 I make lists of what I am going to do.

27 I stand back and think things through.

28 I enjoy social events with other people.

29 I make time for planned relaxation.

30 I need to get everything just right.

INTERPRETING YOUR SCORE

Transfer your scores for individual questions across the following columns of boxes. Each column represents a life skill. Add up the scores in each column and then refer to the interpretations for each life skill below.

A		B		C		D		E		F	
1		2		3		4		5		6	
7		8		9		10		11		12	
13		14		15		16		17		18	
19		20		21		22		23		24	
25		26		27		28		29		30	
TOTAL		TOTAL		TOTAL		TOTAL		TOTAL		TOTAL	

A: Assertiveness
Over 13 You appear to be assertive in your behavior. You are able to express yourself openly and stand up for your rights.
8–13 You could be more assertive.
Below 8 You do not appear to be assertive enough.
See ASSERTIVENESS *pp.82–93.*

B: Managing your time
Over 13 You seem to manage your time well and organize yourself to achieve what you want out of life.
8–13 Your time management could improve.
Below 8 You do not appear to manage your time well and need to improve your skills in this area.
See MANAGING YOUR TIME *pp.94–103.*

C: Rational thinking
Over 13 You seem to understand how your thoughts are affected by your feelings and are able to think matters through in a rational manner
8–13 You could improve your understanding of the relationship between your thoughts and moods.
Below 8 Your thinking habits may be causing your stress.
See RATIONAL THINKING *pp.104–113.*

D: Improving relationships
Over 13 You seem to have positive relationships and a good social support system.
8–13 You could improve the ways in which you use your social network as a way of coping.
Below 8 You appear to have problems in your relationships with other people.
See IMPROVING RELATIONSHIPS *pp.114–125.*

E: Self-care
Over 13 You appear to look after yourself well and understand the need for self-care.
8–13 You could improve your self-care.
Below 8 You are neglecting yourself.
See SELF-CARE *pp.126–139.*

F: Maladaptive
Over 13 You appear to have a number of unhelpful habits in the form of strategies that help you to cope in the short term, but which make you more vulnerable to stress. Often, a combination of procrastination, avoidance, perfectionism, bottling up emotions, and allowing pleasure to be squeezed out of your life can lead to high levels of stress. If you have scored 3 or 4 on any of these questions, turn to the following pages for help.
6   OVERCOMING PROCRASTINATION *p.98*
12   EXPRESSING YOUR FEELINGS *pp.88–89*
18   SELF-CARE *pp.126–139*
24   FEARS AND PHOBIAS *pp.22–23* CHANGE *pp.46–47*
30   CONTROLLING PERFECTIONISM *p.99.*
8–13 You need to be aware of these habits and try to break some of them.
Below 8 You do not appear to have a major problem with these unhelpful habits.

ASSERTIVENESS

Many people find it hard to assert themselves, which limits their ability to cope with everyday demands. Measure your assertiveness skills and target areas for improvement.

Learning how to be assertive will increase your self-confidence and enable you to take control of your own life.

Assertiveness is behavior or skill that helps you communicate, clearly and confidently, your feelings, needs, wants, and thoughts. It is the ability to say no to a request, to state an opinion without being self-conscious, or openly to express emotions such as love and anger. Being assertive comes midway between the two extremes of being passive, where you do not stand up for yourself, and being aggressive, where you bully, dominate, and abuse the rights of others. If you are assertive, you feel confident, and have high self-esteem and a solid sense of your own identity. The messages you give out are, "This is me, this is how I feel, this is what I think, I'm okay and you are okay. I am happy to be me." You feel in control of your life, you do not allow negative feelings to build up, and you are able to maintain positive relationships. Assertiveness skills are learned in childhood and reflect the way your parents, family, and teachers treated you and the messages they conveyed. Assertiveness also develops in a stable social environment where there is love and encouragement that effectually permits you to express yourself and to develop a healthy sense of self-identity.

YOUR BELIEFS AND YOUR RIGHTS

If you do not behave assertively, it may be because you hold a number of deep-rooted beliefs that block assertive behavior. Because these beliefs are largely learned in childhood, they can, in time, be unlearned, but before you can challenge them you need to identify them and accept your rights.

The underlying philosophy of assertiveness training is that all people are equal with the same basic human rights. Like everyone else, you are entitled to say what you think and feel, to change your mind, to say no, or to make mistakes. It is useful occasionally to remind yourself of what your rights are.

Being more assertive entails taking some risks. There is no guarantee that people will respond as you wish. However, there is a good chance that you are over-estimating these risks.

BELIEFS THAT BLOCK ASSERTIVENESS

- It is selfish to say what I want.
- Other people should know what I want.
- People should not discuss their feelings.
- It is wrong to change your mind.
- If I say no people will not like me.
- If I say what I think, I will lose friends.
- I mustn't burden others with my worries.

HOW ASSERTIVE ARE YOU?

Read each of the following statements and choose a score that describes how you think and behave. Add up the total of your scores to gauge how assertive you are.

SCORING
Always 4 • Usually 3 • Sometimes 2 • Never 1

1 I feel comfortable speaking in front of a group.

2 If I am annoyed, I can openly express my anger in front of other people.

3 I can admit that "I don't know," if I lack the appropriate knowledge.

4 If I feel something must change I push for it, even if others resist.

5 I can tell a friend if he or she is doing something that bothers me.

6 When I have done something well I can accept a compliment graciously.

7 I can initiate a conversation with a stranger.

8 I can say no and refuse a request if I do not want to do something.

9 I can touch a friend affectionately if I feel warm toward him or her.

10 I will complain in a store or restaurant if the service is not good enough.

11 I can openly ask a friend for a favor.

12 When somebody criticizes me I can talk about it and learn from it.

13 I believe that I have the right to change my mind.

14 I make time to treat myself.

15 I accept responsibility for myself and my mistakes and do not make excuses.

16 I give compliments and tell people if they have done something that I like.

17 I can express my feelings for people close to me whom I like or love.

18 I will acknowledge that I am scared or worried about something.

19 I make my views known even if others do not always agree.

20 I can ask for and accept constructive criticism.

TOTAL SCORE

INTERPRETATION

Over 60 Good assertiveness
You appear to be assertive in the way you behave with others and express yourself well. However, you may feel more assertive in certain areas of your life than in others. Everyone can always improve assertiveness skills in different areas.

45–60 Moderate assertiveness
You have a mixed pattern of assertive and nonassertive behavior. Identify areas of weakness. Do these involve the way you express your emotions or thoughts to those close to you or to strangers or authority figures? Read the following section carefully.

Below 45 Poor assertiveness
You appear to be unassertive and would benefit from learning new techniques. Read the next section and identify areas of weakness. Ask yourself whether you are usually passive, or if at times you tend to veer toward aggressive behavior.

RECOGNIZING PASSIVE AND ASSERTIVE BEHAVIOR

It is helpful to be able to distinguish between different styles of behavior so you can identify whether you have an assertive behavior style. We are all a mixture of the three styles. Problems arise when we are stuck in a particular style and do not have the ability to change. Examine the three different styles, and see if you recognize yourself.

PASSIVE BEHAVIOR

GENERAL CHARACTERISTICS
You are unable to express your feelings and thoughts, or you express yourself in such an apologetic, self-effacing manner that others can ignore you. People walk all over you. You feel that you have no control over events. Others make decisions for you.

MESSAGE COMMUNICATED
"I don't count. My feelings and thoughts are less important than yours. I'll put up with anything. I'm not okay. You're okay."

SUBCONSCIOUS MESSAGE
"Take care of me and look after my needs telepathically. I am a victim."

GOAL
To appease others and avoid conflict and unpleasantness at all costs.

PAYOFFS
You are praised for being selfless. If things go wrong, as a passive follower, you are rarely blamed. Others protect and look after you. You avoid and postpone conflict.

AGGRESSIVE BEHAVIOR

GENERAL CHARACTERISTICS
You stand up for your own rights and satisfy your own needs in a way that violates others and leaves them feeling devastated. Superiority is maintained by attacking and putting others down.

MESSAGE COMMUNICATED
"This is what I think, what I want, and how I feel. What matters to you is not important to me. I'm okay. You're not okay."

SUBCONSCIOUS MESSAGE
"I'll get you before you have a chance to get me. I'm out for number one."

GOAL
To dominate, to win, to force the other person to lose. To punish.

PAYOFFS
You make others do what you want them to do, which gives you a feeling of being in control. You are likely to secure the material things that you desire. You are less vulnerable.

ASSERTIVE BEHAVIOR

GENERAL CHARACTERISTICS
You express feelings and thoughts openly and directly in ways that are respectful of the rights of others. You recognize their needs and ask for what you want. If refused, you feel saddened, but your opinion of yourself is not shattered.

MESSAGE COMMUNICATED
"This is how I think and feel. How about you? If our needs clash we can discuss our differences. I'm okay. You're okay."

SUBCONSCIOUS MESSAGE
"I won't let you take advantage of me and I won't attack you for being who you are."

GOAL
To communicate your thoughts and feelings clearly, adult to adult.

PAYOFFS
The more you stand up for yourself the higher your self-esteem will be. By expressing emotion directly, resentment will not build up. Anxiety is less evident. Loving others becomes easier.

PRICE
Others make unreasonable demands on you. You are trapped within the image of a "nice person." You repress anger and frustration and diminish your ability to love. Occasionally you may explode in aggression. Internal tension leads to somatic symptoms. Low self-esteem.

BODY MOVEMENTS
Hand-wringing. Hunched shoulders. Covering mouth with hand.

EYE CONTACT
Looking down, evasive.

FACIAL EXPRESSION
Half smile when expressing anger or being criticized. Raised eyebrows in anticipation. Quick-changing features.

SPEECH
Often dull and monotonous. Quiet, often dropping away. Tone may be whining or singsong.

LANGUAGE
Long rambling sentences, making use of fill-in words, such as "er," "but," "sort of." Apologetic: "I'm sorry to bother you," "I wouldn't normally say anything but." Self deprecating: "It's only my opinion," "It's not important," "Oh, it doesn't matter," "It's only me," "I'm useless," "I'm hopeless," "You know me." Use of self command statements: "I should," "I ought to," "I must," "I can't." Defensive.

PRICE
You make enemies and must constantly "watch your back." This takes up valuable energy. You may be prone to fear and a sense of paranoia. Relationships may be based on negative emotions and may be unstable, or you may become isolated as others back away.

BODY MOVEMENTS
Finger-pointing, fists clenched, striding impatiently, leaning forward, crossed arms.

EYE CONTACT
Trying to stare down and intimidate.

FACIAL EXPRESSION
Smiling may become sneering, jaw set firm, scowling when angry.

SPEECH
Very firm, often fast, abrupt, clipped. Fluent, few hesitations, often shouting, rising at the end of sentences. Tone sarcastic or cold.

LANGUAGE
Excessive emphasis on "I." Opinion expressed as fact: "That's a useless way of doing it." Threatening questions: "Haven't you finished yet?," "Why did you do it like that?" Threatening requests: "I want that done now," "Do it this way." Blame: "You made a mess of that." Sarcasm: "You must be joking." Heavy-handed advice: "You should," "You ought to," "You must," "Why don't you...?" Defensive.

PRICE
If you are changing to being more assertive you may lose some old friends who prefer the "old you." There is no guarantee that everything will work out. There is pain involved in being assertive. You are risking change in becoming more true to yourself.

BODY MOVEMENTS
Open hand movements. Upright and relaxed.

EYE CONTACT
Firm and direct without staring.

FACIAL EXPRESSION
Smiling when pleased, frowning when angry. Features relaxed. Appropriate or congruent to mood.

SPEECH
Steady and firm. Not too loud or quiet. Fluent, few hesitations. Tone in the middle range.

LANGUAGE
"I" statements that are brief, clear and to the point. "I like," "I think," "I feel." Opinion expressed as opinion not fact. Suggestions without use of "should": "How about...?" "Would you like ...?" Constructive criticism without blame: "I feel angry when you ignore me." Seeking others' opinions: "How does this fit in with your ideas?" Willingness to explore other solutions: "How can we solve this problem?" Nondefensive.

SIX BASIC ASSERTIVENESS SKILLS

1 BASIC ASSERTIVENESS

This technique involves making a straightforward statement in which you stand up for your rights by making clear your needs, wants, feelings, or opinions.

"I want my book back today, please."

To make your assertion stronger, make the statement short and speak slowly, emphasizing each word. Repeat the statement if necessary, placing special emphasis on key words.

"I still want my book back today."

2 SCRIPTING

If a person repeatedly does something to upset you, this technique will help you to express your feelings without causing resentment. Before you confront the person, write a script of what you are going to say. Be polite, concise, and include the following elements:
• the nature of the problem
• how it affects you
• how you feel about it
• what you want to change.

"When you leave the dishes, it means I must do them. It makes me feel annoyed. I'd like you to clean up after you have eaten, please."

3 BROKEN RECORD TECHNIQUE

Use this technique when you need to be persistent in either resisting the demands of a persuasive individual or when making a request of your own.

• Select a statement and keep repeating it.
• Speak softly and calmly.
• Repeat your statement each time the other person speaks.
• Tolerate silences rather than trying to keep talking.
• Persist – you need to state your case once more than the other person states his or her case.

4 NEGOTIATION

Today sophisticated courses train people in the art of negotiation, but a little tact and foresight is often enough to cope with the difficulties of daily life. The following points are, however, important:
• See the other point of view and acknowledge it. *"I can see this is important to you."*
• Ask for clarification. Try to understand the other person's position, needs, and reasoning.
• Keep calm and breathe slowly.
• Prepare yourself in advance.
• State your view.
• Offer a compromise – don't be stubborn.

5 GIVING PRAISE AND COMPLIMENTS

If you find it difficult to give praise, perhaps it is because you expect people to get things right as a matter of course. Or you may feel uncomfortable giving praise, making it appear sarcastic or overly hesitant. The following hints are worth bearing in mind:
• Pick the right time and place.
• Maintain good eye contact.
• Be brief and clear – don't ramble.
• Use "I" statements: *"I liked…" "I'm pleased with the way you…"*
• Be specific and give details: *"I really liked the meal, especially the cherry pie."*

6 RECEIVING PRAISE

If you feel uncomfortable or foolish when someone gives you a compliment, it might be because you believe it is boastful to accept praise. This can lead to receiving praise nonassertively by making apologetic statements like *"Oh, it was nothing really."* Tips for receiving praise assertively are:
• Listen without interrupting.
• Keep your response short.
• Thank the giver directly: *"Thanks, Mary."*
• Do not put yourself down. Agree with or accept the praise: *"Thanks, Mary. I thought it was a good party, too."*

DEALING WITH CRITICISM

If you are assertive, you can accept criticism and learn from it. Criticism may at times be painful, but it is necessary for self-improvement. One of the disadvantages of being predominantly passive is that you may not learn or benefit from constructive criticism. Rather, your reaction is to readily agree with it – "Yes, you're right. I'm hopeless" – and emotionally drown in a sea of self-reproach. Conversely, if you are locked into an aggressive communication style, you may be impervious to criticism, tending to see it as a personal attack. Your typical reaction might be "How dare you?" and your response is to fight and defend yourself to prove that you are the winner. You do not listen to or learn from the criticism at all.

As with most problems concerned with assertiveness, the way in which you react to criticism is based largely on the script you learned as a child. If your childhood experiences of criticism were of a hurtful rejection, you may find it hard to accept criticism as an adult.

There is a very big difference between criticizing a person's behavior and criticizing his or her personality. If, for example, someone says "You are stupid, why did you do that?" that is a negative label of you as an individual and you will, quite naturally, feel rejected. However, if you are told "That was a stupid thing to do," this is a comment on the way you behaved, and implies that you have the power to change that behavior.

WAYS OF GIVING AND RECEIVING CRITICISM

HOW TO GIVE CONSTRUCTIVE CRITICISM
The way in which you give criticism affects the way it is received. Here are some tips on how to criticize constructively:
- Choose a good time and place, ideally somewhere private.
- Stay calm and speak slowly.
- Focus on behavior, not on undermining personality.
- Acknowledge the positive first. Sandwich a negative comment between two positive comments.
- Do not use labels or insults.

HOW TO RECEIVE CONSTRUCTIVE CRITICISM
ACCEPT THE CRITICISM Accept that we all have faults and make mistakes. Avoid expressing guilt or other negative emotions.

"You are so sloppy."
"Yes, I am sometimes sloppy. but I am trying to be neater."

ASK FOR INFORMATION If you feel that criticism is sound but too general, accept it, but ask for further clarification:

"You messed that up."
"Yes, but which part was the worst?"

HOW TO RECEIVE DESTRUCTIVE CRITICISM
DISAGREE WITH THE CRITICISM If the criticism is unjust, use a calm, assertive disagreement:

"No, I'm not always late."

ASK FOR INFORMATION Ask for clarification of criticisms that are badly expressed:

"Why do you think I'm stupid?"

FOGGING Agree only with the true aspects of the criticism.

"You are lazy, dirty, and sloppy."
"Yes, I am sometimes sloppy."

EXPRESSING YOUR FEELINGS

Learning how to be more open relieves tension and makes you feel healthy and relaxed.

Some people are born with a natural ability to communicate their ideas and feelings to others comfortably. However, if you find it difficult to express yourself, tension and stress may build. The advantage of being in touch with and expressing your feelings is that emotions give motivation, guidance, purpose, and direction to your life. If you can learn to communicate your feelings to others you will feel more alive, with a sharper sense of your own identity. You will also find that tension levels go down, helping you feel relaxed and more healthy. An ability to express your emotions with your partner or close friends will usually deepen and strengthen the relationships. Telling other people how you feel also makes it easier for them to communicate their feelings to you.

UNDERSTANDING EMOTIONS

People deal with emotions in different ways. At one extreme are those who sail through life at the mercy of their feelings, tossed about like a ship with no rudder – "blinded by their emotions." At the other extreme are people who are unaware of their feelings and are governed by their intellect – "blind to their emotions." Both extremes produce their own difficulties, and perhaps the best position to be in is analogous to a sailboat, which is driven by the wind of emotion but has a rudder – rational intellect – to help steer a good course.

There are a number of facts about expressing feelings that are worth considering:

- FAMILY IS A MAJOR INFLUENCE As a young child you can express your feelings openly, spontaneously, and without shame. As you grow up you learn to control and hide those feelings. Traditionally, boys tend to be encouraged to express feelings such as anger and aggression, while girls more commonly express love and fear. Consider how emotions were handled in your family. Were you actively encouraged to express how you felt? Were there particular emotions that were not encouraged? Which emotions do you associate with each of your parents?

- EMOTIONS ARE RELATED TO NEEDS Your three main areas of need are to give and receive love, to make choices and have control, and to understand and communicate. These needs produce both positive and negative emotions. Love is accompanied by feelings of joy, warmth, and affection, while the loss or lack of love leads to sadness and loneliness. If you can make choices and direct events you feel strong and confident, but a loss of control makes you feel frustrated and helpless. If you understand what is happening, you feel calm, relaxed, and safe, but lack of understanding causes fear and confusion.

- DEPTH AND QUALITY OF FEELINGS VARY The depth of your emotional reaction will vary according to the importance you place on the event that causes it. You are likely to feel devastated by the death of someone close, but only mildly irritated at being stuck in a traffic jam. However, occasionally, an apparently trivial event may trigger a backlog of emotional experiences and memories.

You may also experience a complex mixture of emotions at the same time. For example, a severe loss may make you feel sad, angry, and frightened of the future.

- FEELINGS PRODUCE PHYSICAL CHANGES
Although feelings are essentially mental processes, they can bring about real, internal, physiological changes. For example, when you are in love you might feel full of energy, nervousness in the form of butterflies in your stomach, a loss of appetite, and a sense of bubbling over. If you lose love you might feel heavy, lacking in energy, and listless. Similarly, feelings of fear or confusion are often accompanied by trembling, tightening of the muscles, sweating, and increased heart rate.

- THREE LEVELS OF EXPRESSING FEELINGS At the first level you notice and acknowledge to yourself what is going on. For example, you might sigh or be aware of feeling sad. At the second level you express yourself verbally; for example, saying, "I feel hurt by that" or "I feel very warm toward you." At the third level, you release your feelings physically, such as shouting and jumping for joy, crying, trembling, stamping your feet, or slamming a door.

As a child you can express your feelings spontaneously and openly, but as you grow up you learn to control those feelings.

- DISCUSSING YOUR FEELINGS CAN HELP
There is a myth that if you are gripped by an emotion and talk to other people about it, the process will heighten the emotion and make it more likely that you will act irrationally on that emotion. In fact, the reverse is true. By discussing a strong feeling, you release some of the emotion. In this way, you see the feeling more rationally and consequently understand it more easily. Acknowledging an emotion by saying "I feel anxious" can help you to relax.

TUNE IN TO YOUR EMOTIONS

1 MONITOR HOW YOU FEEL

As you go through the day, stop and listen to your body. What is it telling you? A headache may be the result of feeling frightened or overextended. Butterflies in your stomach may be due to feeling anxious or unsafe. Try to select an appropriate adjective to describe the feeling. *"I feel slightly irritated"* or *"I'm feeling angry."*

2 TALK ABOUT YOUR FEELINGS

Once you have become better at recognizing your feelings, make a point of describing them to someone close to you. Try to do this at least once a day. It might be easier to start off with less personal self-disclosures, such as, *"I was really upset by that movie last night,"* moving upward to *"I like you,"* then to *"I feel very close to you,"* and finally *"I love you."*

3 EXPRESS YOURSELF PHYSICALLY

Once you can talk comfortably about your feelings, make an effort to express them physically. Touch somebody you like on the arm as a greeting or parting. Smile, sing, or laugh to show you are happy. Bang a door or stamp your feet if you feel anger about something. If someone's sadness touches you, allow yourself to cry.

SAYING NO

Saying no openly and directly can help boost self-esteem.

If you find it difficult to say no, you probably spend a lot of your time doing things for other people that you would really prefer not to do. This often leads to a gradual buildup of resentment and frustration that may poison friendships and relationships. You probably also feel that you have little control over your time and your life in general. It is like being flooded by water and not being able to turn off the tap. Saying yes to the demands of others when you would rather say no can create stress and tension in your body, which often brings about physical symptoms such as headaches. Saying no is the equivalent of turning off the tap and stopping the flow of external demands or stresses. It puts you in the driver's seat and gives you greater control over your life and time. Saying no directly and openly also helps boost your confidence and self-esteem.

People who have difficulty saying no often share a number of key beliefs. These might include: "Nice people do things for others – to say no would be rude and selfish"; "They are more important than me, so I can't refuse"; "If I say no they will be hurt, angry, or offended and they won't like me any more"; or "I need to feel needed, to be busy, involved, and feel important." If you hold these beliefs you need to identify and challenge them or you will be overloaded.

The inability to say no often stems from two fundamental thinking errors. First, you may be confusing rejecting a request with rejecting the person. There is a big difference: rejecting a request does not mean rejecting the person who made it. Second, you may tend to overestimate the difficulty that the other person will have in accepting the refusal.

"If I refuse their offer, they might never ask me out again."

HOW TO SAY NO AND MEAN IT

1 BE BRIEF Keep your reply short and to the point, and avoid long rambling justifications.

2 BE POLITE Acknowledge the person making the request in your response, saying something like, *"No, I'm sorry, I can't make lunch on Tuesday, but thank you anyhow for asking me."*

3 KEEP CONTROL Soften the abruptness of a direct no by remaining calm, and replying to the request slowly and with warmth.

4 BE HONEST Making a simple statement like *"I'm finding this difficult"* may help you to express difficult feelings honestly and openly.

5 SAY NO AND GO People may interpret lingering as uncertainty, which may cause confusion.

6 PRACTICE Act out in front of a mirror what you might say and do in a situation where you would like to say no, perhaps to extra work or a family duty. Then put it into practice.

Most people are happy to accept an honest no if expressed appropriately. Very often it helps deepen a relationship: when you are honest, it frees the other person to openly express his or her feelings and enables him or her to ask for a favor again without resentment.

You can expect the first time you say no to be the hardest. However, with practice, it will eventually become second nature. Different situations naturally demand a variety of responses, and it is helpful to be aware of a range of techniques of saying no that you can match to a particular event. Very often, the way you are asked to do something can affect the style of your response and you should learn to recognize the tone of the request. For example, a persistent salesperson will receive a different response from a friend in genuine need of help.

There is more than one way to say no.

SIX TECHNIQUES FOR SAYING NO

1 SIMPLE, DIRECT NO
The goal here is to say no without apologizing. The other person has the problem, but you must not allow him or her to pass it on to you.

"No, no, I prefer not to."

A direct no is forceful and can be effective with aggressive salespeople.

2 REFLECTING NO
This technique involves reflecting back the content and feeling of the request, and adding your assertive refusal at the end.

"I know the letters are urgent but I can't go to the post office tonight."

This is a firm and final way of saying no that allows no room for more negotiation.

3 REASONED NO
This method gives very briefly the genuine reason for the refusal.

"I can't mail the letters tonight, because I'm meeting a friend."

You might use this method of refusal if you do not want to offend but have a genuine reason for refusing. It does not open up more negotiation.

4 RAINCHECK NO
This is the way to say no to the present request, without refusing it.

"I can't mail the letters tonight, but I can go in the morning."

This is not a definite no and could be a prelude to negotiation. Use this technique only if you can genuinely fulfill the request later.

5 INQUIRING NO
This is not a definite no and is a genuine invitation to open negotiation.

"Is there any other time you would like me to go?"

You could use this technique if you want to do what is being asked of you, but the timing does not suit you.

6 BROKEN RECORD NO
This method involves repeating a simple statement of refusal over and over again.

"No, I can't go to the post office."
"Oh, please, the letters have to go out tonight."
"No, I can't go to the post office."

This is a good method to use with someone who is persistent.

DEALING WITH ANGER

Suppressing anger causes resentment and tension that can eat away at you.

Anger is a natural, healthy emotional response to hurt, frustration, threat, or loss. If you are able to express your anger appropriately, it can often be a creative force that will motivate you and help you move forward and change your life. There are essentially two different kinds of anger. Healthy, healing anger or annoyance is expressed appropriately at the time it arises, toward the person who triggered it, about the issue that provoked it. However, unhealthy destructive anger, caused by bottling up feelings at the appropriate time, is often expressed too late, to the wrong person, about unrelated issues.

THE PRICE OF BEING "TOO NICE"

If you believe that you should always appear controlled and even-tempered, you may start to suffer. If you never show anger or irritation, other people may find it difficult to express their negative feelings to you, and you will miss out on valuable feedback that helps you develop as a person. Concealing your true feelings may also prevent you from developing intimate relationships. Though unpleasant and painful at the time, an honest fight often brings people closer together. Suppressing your anger also suppresses other emotions, and highs and lows are sacrificed for the average, "same as always" feelings. This can also apply to sexual feelings. Holding in anger can lead to physical and emotional problems including depression, headaches, and stomach ulcers.

In the developed world the overt expression of feelings is generally frowned upon. If you have difficulty expressing anger, this may be because as a child, your natural anger was stifled by controlling parents. Many women also recognize that their parents were more likely to tolerate angry outbursts from the boys in their family. Or perhaps you were hurt by adult anger and now have a fear of the experience repeating itself.

BELIEFS THAT MAY SUPPRESS ANGER

To begin to deal with anger, you need to reassess and identify a number of beliefs that you may have internalized and that prohibit you from expressing anger.

- FEAR OF DEVASTATING OTHERS It is easy to think "If I express my anger, it will completely destroy the other person." Be careful not to overestimate how frail and unable to cope the other person is. If you have an angry outburst, he or she will cope with your anger, although you should be ready for your relationship to change – possibly for the better.

- FEAR OF BEING SEEN TO BEHAVE BADLY If you believe that you should be "nice" at all times and that anger or annoyance is always wrong and inappropriate, your behavior may start to become passive. You will become too ready to comply with other people's wishes, which may lead to a buildup of resentment.

- FEAR OF LOSING CONTROL You are unlikely to lose control if you let out your

Though painful, an honest fight can bring people closer together.

feelings at the right time and appropriately. The more familiar you are with your own anger, the better you will be able to control it. If you overcontrol and repress all anger, when it does break out, you will be unfamiliar with the emotion and are likely to lose control.

■ FEAR OF BEING REJECTED In a formal relationship, anger may lead to a negative response. However, being able to express anger can strengthen personal relationships and make them more durable. You will be seen not as an even-tempered and controlled ideal, but as a real person, with real emotions. Challenge thoughts such as "If I get angry I will be rejected."

■ FEAR OF BEING DESTRUCTIVE Don't be afraid to express anger openly and spontaneously. It often makes other people sit up and notice that you feel strongly about something and can produce positive, constructive changes. Confront thoughts such as "Getting angry is destructive and negative."

■ FEAR OF REPERCUSSIONS The belief that other people will seek revenge on you for your anger often originates in childhood, if anger was strictly punished by parents or other adults. However, in adult life, the risk of repercussions for an outburst of anger is far less than the problems you may cause yourself by suppressing your feelings.

LEARN TO MANAGE ANGER

1 DON'T BOTTLE IT UP
If you feel irritated, talk to somebody about your feelings and reactions when they occur. This reduces tension. By expressing minor irritations, you can avoid a buildup of anger that might end in rage or an explosive outburst.

2 OWN YOUR FEELINGS
Claim your anger and do not blame others for your feelings. Say "I feel really angry when. " and not "You make me angry." Accept that it is your own beliefs and not other people that make you feel angry.

3 JUDGE YOUR LEVEL OF ANGER
Be aware of levels of anger, from mild irritation to blind rage. Notice physical changes, from slight muscle tension to rapid breathing, increased heart rate, trembling, and feeling hot and flushed.

4 UNDERSTAND THE CAUSES
The main causes of anger are rigid beliefs. Examine your "shoulds," "ought tos," and "musts." How rigid are they? The more flexible your beliefs, the less likely you are to feel frustrated and become angry. Ask yourself if the situation is triggering feelings from the past.

5 PHYSICALLY EXPRESS THE FEELING
Relearn some childlike actions for diffusing tension without hurting others: stamp your feet, hit a cushion, scream and shout. If you cannot vent your anger spontaneously, it may come out in other inappropriate ways – on the road, kicking the dog, or shouting at the children.

6 FORGIVE
After you have expressed your anger, try to wipe the slate clean, forget the incident, forgive and move on. If you have overreacted to the situation, apologize. Accept and understand the anger in others. Are you taking it too personally? We are all imperfect humans struggling to manage complex emotions.

MANAGING YOUR TIME

Never having enough time to do the things you want to do causes tension and puts strain on relationships. Learning how to organize your time and delegate can help to relieve the pressure.

Plan relaxation time for yourself into your daily schedule. If you feel relaxed, you will be better able to cope with everyday demands.

Time is the most important and valuable resource we have, but in order to exploit it to the fullest, we need to manage it properly. How often do you say to yourself "There is just not enough time in the day to finish everything"; "I've got far too much to do"; "I have not gotten anything done today"; or "I'm not spending enough time on the things that are really important to me, such as my family and friends"? The way you spend your time determines the quality of your life. If you do not manage your time successfully you may start to feel you are not in control of events, making you frustrated, dissatisfied, and stressed.

The central principle of time management is to spend your time doing the things that you value or that help you to achieve your goals. It means making time to enjoy what you do,

as well as getting through what you have to do. The principles of time management apply equally to people of all ages, from children in school, to mothers at home with babies, to ambitious executives with full agendas.

Good time management depends on being realistic about what you know you must do within a certain time period, knowing what you want to do, and organizing your life to achieve a balance between the two. You need to keep work in perspective and plan time to relax on your own at home or with family and friends. You also need to identify and prioritize your most productive areas to achieve a maximum output in a minimum of time.

According to the 80/20 rule, also known as the Pareto Principle, 80 percent of your effort brings only 20 percent of your rewards, while the remaining 20 percent of effort brings 80 percent of your rewards. By identifying and concentrating on the 20 percent of effort you need to bring the 80 percent of rewards, you can greatly increase your efficiency.

Focus on your priorities.

HOW DO I SPEND MY TIME?

Divide each day into 15-minute intervals and at the end of each hour categorize how the previous hour was spent. List your findings and summarize the results, taking into account the following questions:

- Do the time allocations reflect your priorities?

- Which items take up large parts of your time and make little contribution to your overall goals?

- What proportion of time do you spend working, relaxing, socializing?

- Is the balance between leisure time and work as you would wish it to be?

THE KEYS TO GOOD TIME MANAGEMENT

1 KNOW YOUR GOALS IN LIFE

Identify the activities you value most and your main goals at work and at home. These goals are the map you need to direct your life and schedule your time. Break down your main goals into smaller, more manageable tasks.

2 RANK PRIORITIES

Ask yourself how important a particular task is to you. Activities can be ranked according to their importance. Try identifying the activities that produce the greatest reward. Give these activities priority over others.

3 WRITE DOWN YOUR PLANS

A written plan enables you to take a more detached view of your commitments. Keep a diary of important dates and tasks to be done. A daily "to do" list can give direction and a sense of achievement once tasks have been accomplished.

4 DELEGATE TASKS

Trying to do everything yourself is often a major cause of stress. Take a look at your schedule and work out what you can hand to somebody else to do. You can still monitor other people's progress and maintain a level of control.

5 WORK OUT A SYSTEM

Disorganization makes work and wastes time. Organize your environment so that everything has its place. Keep a note pad and calendar by the phone, and set up a filing system for bills. Establish a daily routine.

6 DO IT NOW – NOT LATER

By putting off today's tasks until tomorrow you are simply storing up work for yourself. Ask yourself, *"Why am I putting it off?"* Set realistic deadlines for each day and then do your best to keep to them.

7 ALLOW SLACK IN TIMETABLE

Never overfill your time-table. Always allow some slack. Then, if there is an emergency, you can accommodate it. If you know that your time is not stretched to the limit you will feel less stressed. Plan time for rest and relaxation.

8 LEARN TO SAY NO

If you cannot say no to the demands of others, you will end up being a servant to their priorities, never able to say or do what you want. Stay in control of your own time, and say no to timewasting and unnecessary activities.

9 ONE THING AT A TIME

You may have many things to do, but you cannot do them all at once, especially since important tasks usually require energy and concentration. You will find it less stressful if you can finish one task before starting another.

10 KNOW YOUR PRIME TIME

Identify when you work best and plan that time for your most important or demanding tasks. For most people this is early in the morning. Allocate undemanding tasks to times when your energy may be low.

11 YOU'RE NOT PERFECT

If you are a perfectionist, you may become bogged down in detail and find it difficult to vary your speed according to priorities. Learn to assess the situation in advance, so you can work within set time limits.

12 KEEP A BALANCE

Planning time for work, rest, and play will help maintain your health and enthusiasm and allow you to keep a balanced perspective. Break your routine and plan time to relax during the day. Take regular vacations.

GOAL PLANNING

Goals give your life direction and improve motivation and performance.

Identify your goals and work toward them.

As humans, we are goal-directed creatures, constantly striving for meaning and significance in our lives. We all need a purpose, a role, something to work toward, and even the smallest goals are enough to give life meaning. Studies into the progress of people who have spent time living in a stressful environment, such as prison, prove that those who are best equipped to cope are those who have goals or who can create specific goals to work toward. Similarly, in studies of successful people, the characteristic common to all of them is that they work toward predetermined goals. Stress is often caused by one of the following:

- Not having any clear direction or objective to work toward.
- Having too many goals all making demands on your limited time
- Having conflicting goals – for example, wanting to do well at work and earn a lot of money so you can improve your standard of living, but also wanting to have more leisure time at home with your family.
- Finding yourself working toward goals that are not really yours – for example, training at medical school because your parents always wanted you to be a doctor.

Given that goals give direction to your life and improve your motivation and performance, it is curious that so few people set themselves personal goals. This may be simply because they do not know how to, or they may not realize the importance of setting objectives to work toward. For some people, this inability to set goals stems from a deep-seated fear of failure. Once a goal is set, you either succeed or fail in achieving it. However, people who have a fear of failing do not realize that failure is an essential part of success. If you have not learned the value of failure, you cannot hope to be successful.

Before you can attempt to identify and set your own goals, it helps if you can clarify exactly what is important in your life. Most of the time we are so busy tackling our day-to-day chores that

FREE YOUR THINKING

Find out what you value most in your life by answering the following questions within the allotted times.

- Which five values do you hold most dear e.g., honesty, reliability? (45 seconds)
- What are the three most important goals in your life? (45 seconds)
- How would you spend your time if you had only six months to live? (30 seconds)
- What would you change about your life if you suddenly became a millionaire? (30 seconds)
- What would you choose as an epitaph to sum up your life? (30 seconds)
- What activities give you the greatest feelings of fulfillment? (60 seconds)
- What have you always wanted to do but not dared to try? (30 seconds)

we never stop to consider exactly how we are spending our time. It is all too easy to slip into a routine and for weeks to pass by in which you seem to achieve nothing. You probably feel there are certain things you should be doing, but unless you identify these you are unlikely to achieve them. Make a point of breaking your routine and put aside some time to set yourself some realistic goals for the coming year. By writing down your goals, you make them visible and tangible. You can see them in front of you, and this makes it more difficult for you to procrastinate and put off doing them. Writing down a goal also entails commitment. If you are reluctant to write it down, you are leaving your options open so that if you do not achieve it you can always say to yourself, "I never really meant to do that anyway."

Take time to plan what you want out of life.

EIGHT STEPS TOWARD ACHIEVING YOUR GOALS

1 BRAINSTORM
Write down all the things you want out of life in the next year and five years, however unrealistic these may seem. Include your dreams as well as goals. Make three separate lists for work, home, and your leisure time.

2 RECONSIDER
Check your list of goals for incompatability or unattainability. Don't plan to study for a degree in your spare time as well as spend more time at home. Aim to win your local golf championship, but don't plan to win an Olympic gold medal.

3 ORDER YOUR LIST
Look at your list and decide which are the most important goals in each of the three categories. Rank them in terms of priority. Then decide which of all the goals is the most important for you to achieve.

4 BE SPECIFIC
Rewrite the goals in specific, measurable language, preferably observing a time limit.

"I want to write a story"

will become

"By the end of December I will have finished writing a 5,000-word short story."

5 WRITE AN ACTION PLAN
For each goal draw up a list of the steps that you need to take to achieve it. Thus, to write a short story the action plan may be:
- to enroll on a course
- buy equipment
- create a work space
- set aside regular time.

6 IDENTIFY OBSTACLES
Decide what may get in the way and look for solutions. If, for example, you feel that people will make too many demands on your time, resolve this by setting aside specific time in your calendar and meshing it with family and work.

7 REWARD YOURSELF
Rewards will boost your motivation. Think of something you really want, and promise to treat yourself if you achieve a difficult goal:

"If I finish the story by Christmas, I will treat myself to some new software."

8 VISUALIZE THE END RESULT
Create a clear picture in your mind of the situation when you have finally achieved your goal.

"I will get bound copies of the finished story, and my friends and family will be able to read it."

OVERCOMING PROCRASTINATION

Procrastination means putting something off that you know you need to do. We are all guilty of saying "I'll do it later," or "I must get around to that." But some people put things off to such an extent that they never do much at all, causing stress and anxiety to build up.

People who procrastinate are deliberately avoiding confronting their fears. Procrastination flourishes under two conditions:
- When a task is not urgent and there is plenty of time to do it in the future.
- If there is something you would rather be doing now.

Behind these conditions are several factors:

- FEAR OF FAILURE You may leave it until the very last minute and then say, "I didn't have enough time to do it." By doing this, you are giving yourself an excuse, and you may be protecting yourself from the reality that your best might not have been good enough.
- FEAR OF SUCCESS If you are too successful, people might expect more next time.
- FEAR OF REJECTION OR INTIMACY By never getting around to inviting your friends to dinner, you manage to keep a safe emotional distance between yourself and others.
- LACK OF COMMITMENT You may simply not consider the task important enough.

EIGHT WAYS OF TACKLING PROCRASTINATION

1 MAKE A LIST
List the tasks that you put off in all areas of your life. Select one and note down your excuses for putting it off. Go through the following steps and carry it out now.

2 LIST THE PROS AND CONS
Draw up two columns on a sheet of paper and list the advantages and disadvantages of putting off the task.

3 JUST DO IT
Your expectations are usually worse than reality. Like getting into a cold swimming pool, tackling unpleasant situations slowly is much more painful than just jumping straight in.

4 PLAN IT
Put the task in your calendar or on your "to do" list. Make it part of your routine so you do not have to think about it. If you start the day with the least pleasant task, the day gets better.

5 SLICE IT UP
If the task is overwhelming, do it a piece at a time. Mix the task up with more pleasurable activities and carry it out bit by bit, regularly, and often until it is completed.

6 THINK POSITIVELY
Write down and challenge any negative thoughts you have about the task you are putting off. Lower your expectations. Don't aim to be perfect.

7 PLAN REWARDS
Reward yourself once you have achieved your goal. Make yourself a hot drink, watch your favorite television program, or treat yourself to a little present.

8 WORK TO DEADLINES
Say to yourself, *"I will have this done by…"* Make yourself accountable by announcing your deadlines to family, friends, or colleagues.

CONTROLLING PERFECTIONISM

A perfectionist is a person who has to get everything just right. Most of us reach a stage in a task where putting in more effort will only bring very marginal gains. We recognize that this is the time to stop and focus on something more profitable. A perfectionist, however, has difficulty varying standards according to factors such as time available, consequences of not being able to stop working, and the effort needed. Perfection is an unobtainable illusion guaranteed to make you feel like a failure.

The advantage of perfectionism is that occasionally you produce fine work. The disadvantages are that you are likely to feel tense and find it difficult to relax, you are likely to be critical of yourself and others (adversely affecting relationships), and you are likely to be inclined to avoid challenges or taking risks.

Perfectionism conceals a number of deep, unrecognized fears. As a perfectionist you are motivated by a fear of failure. In failing to reach a goal, you feel you have failed as a person, making you self-critical. However well you perform, you are never satisfied and constantly strive for better results. You may also tend to keep too tight a rein on your emotions for fear of showing vulnerability or losing control. In contrast, people with a healthy pursuit of excellence are motivated by enthusiasm, are happy with themselves, are not afraid of failing, and can show vulnerability.

BENEFITS OF BEING "IMPERFECT"

- You learn from your mistakes. By doing something wrong, you can learn from the experience and get it right next time.

- Most people find that they are more comfortable with "imperfect," vulnerable people than with "perfect" saints.

- If you are afraid that you might make a mistake, you run the risk of becoming paralyzed into inaction, frightened to attempt anything new.

FOUR WAYS OF OVERCOMING PERFECTIONISM

1 LIST THE PROS AND CONS
Show that perfectionism does not in fact help you, by listing the advantages and disadvantages of perfectionism and how they affect your life.

2 SET DEADLINES
Identify a task and set a time limit for it. Instead of saying, *"I am going to write a letter,"* say, *"I've got 15 minutes to write this letter, so I'll keep it short."*

3 DISCUSS YOUR WEAKNESSES
Confide in close friends or family and tell them if you feel inadequate or nervous in a situation. Treat this as a challenge. Dare to be average and admit it.

4 SAVOR THE MOMENT
Try to focus more on the process rather than its outcome. Stop and enjoy the here and now, rather than concentrating on the end result.

DELEGATION

Delegation means getting things done, or achieving goals, through the efforts of other people. It is an essential skill whether you are managing an office, a business, or a home. One recent study showed that 97 percent of managers' time was spent on "doing things" rather than managing, while only 3 percent of their time was devoted to tasks that the managers were uniquely qualified to perform. Delegation involves giving other people the authority to take responsibility for tasks and not just passing on all the unpleasant jobs to somebody else. The underlying principle is that any advancement or progress depends on producing results beyond your own capabilities – you will never make progress if you have to do everything yourself. An inability to delegate means holding on to the idea that you can do it all yourself. This often leads to your feeling under pressure, working longer hours, never having any spare time, and feeling isolated. The effect on others around you is that they feel impotent as they have not been given authority or responsibility and so are prevented from developing skills in their own right. This frequently leads to resentment, poor morale, and a lack of team spirit. This can apply equally in a business organization or a family.

There are a number of reasons why people find it difficult to delegate. Most of these are underlying, often unrecognized, fears and insecurities centered around the following emotions:

- GUILT "I can't ask Jane to do it for me; she already has her hands full."
- FEAR OF FAILURE "What if Pete does it wrong? That will make me look bad."
- ENVY, OR FEAR OF BECOMING INVISIBLE "What if he succeeds too well? They might think he is better at his job than I am."
- FEAR OF LETTING GO This is also known as the "martyr syndrome": "I'll do it myself and feel virtuous – nobody ever helps me."

Very often people are unsure of what they can usefully and effectively pass on to somebody else to do.

POSSIBLE CAUSES OF AND SOLUTIONS TO POOR DELEGATION

If you have problems delegating, the following points may help you think more rationally.

- *If she's better than me I will become dispensable.* Be grateful. Nobody can be good at everything.

- *She is already busy. I mustn't overload her.* Have an overview of her priorities.

- *What if she fails? It will make me look bad.* Train her. Anticipate her mistakes. She will benefit in the long term.

- *I could do the job better myself.* Don't try to be a perfectionist; let things go.

- *I do not want to look like a tyrant, or lazy.* Explain why you are delegating.

- *She might refuse to do what I ask.* You can ask and she can refuse.

- *I'll do it. I prefer "doing things" to managing.* Fine, but think how this will affect your limited time.

- *It would be quicker to do it myself.* At the moment, but consider the longer term.

- *I'll do it myself. It makes me feel virtuous.* Beware of becoming resentful and manipulatively instilling guilt in others.

The following list includes four categories of task that can usefully be delegated:

- Jobs that others can do just as well as you.
- Jobs that you are not skilled to do yourself.
- Jobs that could help others learn and grow.
- Routine tasks.

Management manuals describing the job of a manager at work emphasize the importance of delegation. It is often said that a good manager will not ask him- or herself "What should I delegate?" but rather, "What should I not delegate?" If you cannot think of a good reason to hold on to a task, then delegate it, and leave yourself time to think, plan, and manage. A good way to work out for yourself the type of tasks you could be delegating is to make a list of tasks, at work or at home, that you yourself have completed recently or that are ongoing, and mark which ones you feel you could have delegated to other people but have not. In each case identify a person who you know would like to do the task, who would benefit from the task, or who has the expertise to do the task. Now try to identify the obstacles or fears that have prevented you from delegating. For example, you might have just painted your house yourself because you think a painter would have been too expensive. Now think of what you paid by not delegating in terms of your time and the equipment you had to buy.

You will never make progress if you try to do everything yourself.

HOW TO DELEGATE EFFECTIVELY

1 GIVE CLEAR INSTRUCTIONS

This does not mean telling the person exactly how to do something, but it does mean outlining what needs doing, explaining why it needs doing, and setting standards. It is also important to set firm deadlines.

2 PASS ON AUTHORITY AND RESPONSIBILTY

- Delegate the entire task to one person, not half a task.
- Provide the necessary resources.
- Do not relinquish complete control. Be careful not to abandon the person to the task.
- Stay in touch and give support.

3 MAKE SURE THE TASK IS UNDERSTOOD

Discuss the task with the person you want to delegate to. Make sure that he or she has the right skills and is happy about taking it on. It is important that he or she does not feel "put upon."

4 MONITOR PROGRESS

Arrange regular updates. Supervise and support, but do not keep looking over the person's shoulder. Give advice without interfering. It is good to give praise in public, but if you have to criticize, do so in private.

5 ALLOW AUTONOMY AND CREATIVITY

Give the person to whom you are delegating enough space and responsibility to take his or her own decisions. This makes doing the job easier and more pleasant.

6 GIVE FEEDBACK AND PRAISE

When the task is completed, go over it with the person, giving specific comments and praise, so that the person can learn from it. Grant the delegatee full credit for his or her accomplishments.

REDUCING HURRY SICKNESS

Type A behavior can lead to stress-related illnesses.

Our expectations of modern society are that everything should be instant from travel to information and even fast food. As the pace of life has speeded up, however, the incidence of certain forms of stress-related illness such as coronary heart disease, stomach ulcers, and strokes has also increased. Research indicates that a particular personality type, the so-called type A, is more likely to develop stress-related illnesses. This personality factor appears to be independent of other traditional risk factors, such as high blood pressure, age, or smoking, and represents a cluster of traits that includes the following four patterns of behavior:

- COMPETITIVENESS – the need to achieve.
- HURRY SICKNESS – a sense of time urgency.
- HOSTILITY – a disproportionate sense of frustration if progress is impeded.
- JOYLESS STRIVING – always on the go, taking on many projects at once.

The opposite of type A behavior is type B. Type B personalities are relaxed, unhurried, nonaggressive, and noncompetitive.

ASSESS YOUR TYPE A BEHAVIOR

Answer the following questions and then total up your score to see if you are a type A personality.

SCORING
Always 5 • Usually 4 • Sometimes 3 • Rarely 2 • Never 1

1 Are you punctual for appointments?

2 Are you very competitive?

3 How often do you feel rushed?

4 Do you get aggressive if frustrated?

5 Do you get impatient if kept waiting?

6 Do you interrupt when others speak?

7 Do you push yourself and others hard?

8 Do you hide your personal feelings?

9 Do you try to do many things at once?

10 Are you eager to get things done?

11 Do you talk, walk, and eat quickly?

12 Do you focus too much on work.

INTERPRETATION

Over 40 High-scoring type A
Your "driven" lifestyle is likely to put you under increasing pressure and cause signs of stress.

30–40 Moderate type A
You appear to work hard for success, but be careful not to push yourself too much.

Below 30 Toward type B
You appear to take life easy and are unlikely to suffer from type -A-induced stress.

It is thought that type A behavior leads to excessive discharge of the stress hormones noradrenaline, adrenaline, and cortisol, resulting in excessive insulin in the blood. This can mean that it takes three or four times longer than normal to get rid of dietary cholesterol after meals. A potential result is narrowing of the blood vessels, together with increased deposits of the clotting element in the blood, which may lead to heart disease.

To find out if your personality puts you into the type A category, try the questionnaire on the opposite page. If you have a high score this represents an increased risk of stress-related illnesses. Go through the points below one by one and put them into practice. With the right help, research suggests that type A personalities can learn to alter their behavior, consequently reducing the risk of ill health without impairing performance.

EIGHT WAYS TO MANAGE TYPE A BEHAVIOR

1 SLOW DOWN
Be aware of your obsessive time-directed lifestyle and slow down. Deliberately walk and eat more slowly. Make sure you sit down to eat your meals. Try to schedule fewer activities each day and discipline yourself to allow time to get to places without rushing.

2 SET ASIDE TIME FOR YOURSELF
Build into your daily and weekly schedule stress-free periods when you deliberately try to relax. This might include a 20-minute walk in the park at lunchtime or a five-minute break in the morning when you do a quick relaxation exercise.

3 ONE THING AT A TIME
Instead of trying to do many different things at once, concentrate on one task at a time and complete it before moving on to the next. Do not take on too much work. Know your limit and say no. Don't be a perfectionist.

4 DON'T WATCH THE CLOCK
Give yourself short time-breaks when you use no clocks and make an effort to lose your sense of time. Take your watch off for part of the day or the weekend. Allow yourself to break the habit of always being on time. Miss a few deadlines.

5 TAKE UP HOBBIES
Commit yourself to absorbing active hobbies such as gardening, sailing, and walking, to broaden your horizons. Also try to engage in uncompetitive, unimportant trivial pursuits just for fun.

6 EXPRESS HOW YOU FEEL
Talk to others about your feelings rather than bottling them up. Take time to have a chat to somebody about nothing in particular. Thank others and show your appreciation when somebody has done something for you.

7 MANAGE YOUR HOSTILITY
Keep a diary of situations that make you angry, such as thwarted goals, insults, or threats. This will help you identify provocative situations in advance. Challenge your "should" thoughts. Replace them with calmer thoughts.

8 UNDERSTAND THE REASONS
Ask yourself why you constantly need to achieve and prove yourself to feel good. Think back to your childhood. Was your parents' approval linked to how successful you were? What do you now value most in life?

RATIONAL THINKING

*Many stress-related problems occur as a result of distorted thinking.
By understanding more about the relationship between thoughts and
feelings you can equip yourself better to challenge these thoughts.*

*Learning to think logically
and rationally helps develop
a positive approach to life.*

The way you think and the way you feel are closely connected. In fact, you feel the way you do now because of the thoughts you are thinking at the moment. Imagine that you are walking down the street and are passed by an acquaintance who does not acknowledge you or say hello. You might think, "How dare she snub me like that" and feel angry as a result. Alternatively, you might think, "I must have done something to upset her – maybe she doesn't like me," resulting in guilt and worry. If you think, "She looks preoccupied. I hope she's okay," you may feel concern. This same event, interpreted in three different ways, with three different sets of thoughts, can lead to three different feelings. This shows that it is not events that cause your feelings, but the way you interpret them.

A DOWNWARD SPIRAL OF THOUGHTS

When we are stressed or depressed, we have a built-in selective bias to attend to negative thoughts and images from the past, which affects our perception of the present and future. In one experiment, words were

THE EFFECTS OF THOUGHTS AND FEELINGS

Feelings, or moods, are created by thoughts about events, not by the events themselves. If you interpret an event positively, you feel happy, but negative thoughts may result in your feeling unhappy, frightened, or angry. Your interpretation of events is based on previous experience.

EVENT
*You are in the dentist's
waiting room, about to be
called in to have a filling.*

THOUGHTS
*"I hate coming to the dentist's.
It wouldn't be so bad if the
last filling had been okay. I
hope the injection will work
this time. Last time, when the
dentist drilled into the tooth I
felt everything – the pain was
excruciating."*

MOOD
*"I know as soon as the nurse calls
my name I am going to wish the
ground could open up. I feel really
anxious and blue. I didn't sleep
well for worrying about what
might happen. I'll feel much
happier when it is all over."*

flashed up on a screen at a subliminal level, and it was noticed that people who are depressed picked out more negative words, such as "sad" and "death," than people who are not suffering from depression. People can "think" themselves into a depression or panic in a downward spiral of negative thoughts, where each thought feeds on the last one. For example, you may feel fed up because you think that a party you have just given did not go well. Because you are feeling low, you may then start to think you are not a good host. This thought might trigger a selection of other distorted thoughts and images about other negative situations in the past. You start thinking that you are not a very good person, and before you know it, you are feeling deeply depressed. Such spirals of thoughts and feelings are common and, if you want to break the pattern, you need to be aware of what is happening and learn how to challenge and replace the negative thoughts.

PRINCIPLES OF RATIONAL THINKING

There are a number of principles behind rational thinking that it helps to be aware of:

• THE WAY YOU THINK AFFECTS YOUR MOODS
The major factor in determining mood is the way you interpret events. If a snake slithered under your door, you might think it was a poisonous snake and feel fear, turning to panic. However, if you were a snake expert and recognized it as a harmless grass snake, your interpretation would be different and you would remain calm. Thus, the same event can lead to different reactions depending on how you have learned to think, according to previous experience.

• INFORMATION CHANGES YOUR THINKING
The more information you have about a situation, the less likely you are to be frightened by it. In this way, the first time you experience a panic attack you may have drastic thoughts like "I'm having a heart attack" or "I'm going crazy." but as you learn more about panic you realize that the symptoms are due to a surge of adrenaline and, though unpleasant, are harmless.

> "There is nothing either good or bad, but thinking makes it so."
> W. SHAKESPEARE

• YOUR MOOD AFFECTS THE WAY YOU THINK
Your attention tends to be directed according to your mood. If you think back over your past, when you are feeling low, you tend to remember all the bad things that have happened to you. Similarly if you are feeling happy, your memory will be slanted to recall positive events. This is why our thinking and mood can so easily spiral down in either an anxious or a depressive vicious circle. In effect, a depressed mood is based on an inaccurate, filtered perception of reality.

• EVERYONE IS PRONE TO DISTORTED THINKING
We have all experienced negative moods, based on thoughts that we later recognize to be untrue. After the breakup of a relationship, for example, you may feel no one will ever be attracted to you again. However, as soon as you meet someone new, your feelings change and you wonder how you could ever have had such negative, distorted thoughts.

• BE AWARE OF DISTORTED THINKING If you are aware that your views can become distorted, it is possible to change your manner of thinking and your mood. You can train yourself deliberately to step back and analyze your thoughts. If these thoughts are biased or distorted you can learn to challenge them before they begin to spiral downward.

CHALLENGING DISTORTED THINKING

Recognizing distorted thinking improves your ability to cope.

When you are stressed and under pressure, you are particularly prone to misinterpret events and see things in a distorted or irrational way. A vicious circle evolves, whereby the more anxious or depressed you are, the more irrational your thoughts become – and the more irrational your thoughts, the worse you feel. Before you can break this cycle, you need to be aware of what is happening and why. Research has shown that there are a number of recognized types of distorted thinking that produce irrational thoughts.

■ ALL-OR-NOTHING THINKING If you are prone to all-or-nothing thinking, you think in absolutes with no middle ground. Everything is either black or white, with no shades of gray. If a situation falls short of being perfect, you see it as a total failure and the resulting feelings are equally extreme. You may condemn yourself or others completely on the basis of a single event. You tend to use general labels when you talk, making statements such as "He's completely hopeless," "I'm just not up to it, I'm useless," or "I'm a total failure."

■ AWFULIZING OR CATASTROPHIZING If you catastrophize, you tend to magnify and exaggerate the importance of events and how awful and unpleasant they will be, overestimating the possibility of disaster. If you have one setback, however small, you will tend to see it as the beginning of a never-ending pattern of defeat. You might think, "Whatever can go wrong, will go wrong."

■ PERSONALIZING If you personalize, this means you take responsibility and blame yourself for any unpleasant event, even if it has little or nothing to do with you. If something bad happens you instantly think that you are to blame. Personalization leads to feelings of guilt, shame, and inadequacy. You often say, "It's all my fault."

■ NEGATIVE FILTER If you have a negative filter on your thoughts, you focus on negative details, ignoring or misinterpreting the positive aspects of a situation. If you have done a good job, you filter out and reject the positive comments and focus on negative comments, saying to

IDENTIFY THINKING DISTORTIONS

- Keep a planner linking your thoughts to your mood. Divide your page up under the following headings: Date and time, Description of situation, Mood level 0–10, What I was thinking, Type of thought, Rational challenges.

- When you notice a disturbing change in your mood, note the time, date, and triggering event. Rate your mood on a 10–point scale where 0 is fine and 10 is either extremely depressed or anxious.

- Write down the thoughts that have run through your head. This is not easy; it requires the ability to stand back and consider what you are thinking.

- Try to identify thinking distortions.

- Compose more rational challenges to your distorted thoughts and see how this affects your mood.

yourself "That doesn't count" or "That wasn't good enough" and remember only negative comments. You focus on your weaknesses and forget your strengths, and tend to look on the dark side – "I can see all the mistakes. I did a bad job. I'm not very good at decorating."

- JUMPING TO CONCLUSIONS You make negative interpretations when there are no facts to support your conclusions. You start "mind reading," reaching arbitrary conclusions about other people and reacting negatively without checking the facts. You are inclined to "fortune telling," predicting that things will go badly – "I saw her out with a man – she must be having an affair."
- FIXED RULES ("SHOULDISM") You tend to live by fixed rules and expectations, regularly using the words "should," "ought to," "must," "have to," and "can't." The more rigid your views, the more disappointed you feel. If the statements are directed at yourself, you will

feel guilty, frustrated, and depressed. If they are directed against others, you are likely to feel frustrated and angry – "He should know I hate fish."

Step back and think about what you are thinking.

CHALLENGING YOUR THOUGHTS

When something happens, you identify the event and then react to it either irrationally or rationally. If you have irrational thoughts, your feelings and behavior are likely to be abnormal and disturbed. However, by challenging your negative, irrational thoughts with rational thoughts, you can steer your feelings and behavior onto a more steady course. With practice, you will soon learn how to identify, recognize, and challenge your irrational thoughts as soon as they occur. This is called emotional sequencing.

EMOTIONAL SEQUENCING

You are in the car with your husband. You warn him of an oncoming car, and he reacts angrily.

IRRATIONAL THOUGHT	THINKING DISTORTION	CHALLENGING THOUGHTS
"I have made him angry and upset – it's all my fault."	Personalizing	"He had a headache that was making him irritable."
"I nag him too much. I should be a better wife. I hate myself."	All-or-nothing thinking Fixed rules ("shouldism")	"I do nag sometimes, but it is not a reason for him to hate me."
"He hates me."	Jumping to conclusions Awfulizing All-or-nothing thinking	"I have no grounds for believing this. It is not as awful as I think. I know he loves me."
"He's going to be angry with me for the rest of the day now."	Jumping to conclusions All-or-nothing thinking	"Why should he be? It wasn't serious, and he's not petty."
"I suppose it was better to warn him than risk an accident."	None	This was a rational thought

COMMON IRRATIONAL BELIEFS

This chart highlights nine deep-seated, irrational beliefs, which we initially learn in childhood and which have been identified as prime culprits in creating irrational thinking and emotional distress. We may all hold some of these beliefs, but problems occur when these beliefs are held too rigidly. Examine the chart and identify which beliefs you hold more than others.

1 I NEED TO BE LIKED

The approval of others is not essential. In order to live your life fully you need to express yourself, and this will occasionally mean upsetting others. If you constantly try to avoid disapproval, you will take on a passive role and your self-esteem will plummet. You cannot please everyone.

2 I MUST BE SUCCESSFUL

Are you constantly striving to achieve and be successful? If you are a "driven" individual, you may find that your life becomes unbalanced with not enough time to relax. You will never achieve enough and are likely to feel dissatisfied. It is important to ease up and accept that "failing" is sometimes helpful and instructive.

3 IT'S A DISASTER WHEN THINGS GO WRONG

If you hold the belief that life should be fair, just, and ordered, which it is not, and geared toward satisfying your needs, you will be constantly disappointed, frustrated, and angry. Behind this belief are the key words "should," "ought to," "have to," and "must."

4 THE WORST IS GOING TO HAPPEN

Excessive worry about situations beyond your control is unproductive. Be aware of the tendency to "catastrophize" and watch out for thoughts such as: *"Wouldn't it be terrible if…"* Even the worst possible outcome is often not as bad as we imagine.

5 MY MOODS ARE RULED BY OUTSIDE FORCES

This belief leads to a passive acceptance of what fate brings, when, in reality, you can very often play a large part in controlling your own destiny. We can all influence our own moods, feelings, and behavior, but first we have to take responsibility for ourselves.

6 IT IS EASIER TO AVOID DIFFICULT SITUATIONS

Avoidance leads to lack of confidence and an inability to learn from experience. Avoidance is caused by fear of failure and by the belief that failure is bad. If you avoid challenges and always take the easy option, you learn less and your confidence will be gradually eroded.

7 I CANNOT CHANGE THE WAY I AM

You believe the past is all-important, so if something once affected you, it cannot be altered. Thoughts such as, *"That's just the way I am. I'll never change,"* are suggestive of this belief. Although the past has an effect on our behavior, we can learn new skills and develop as people.

8 PEOPLE SHOULD BEHAVE PROPERLY

You have a rigid "should" belief about how people should behave. When people's behavior does not correspond with your expectations, you blame and condemn those people and view them as completely awful. You have difficulty appreciating how they perceive the world.

9 I CAN BE HAPPY BY DOING NOTHING

Do you find yourself saying, *"I'm bored,"* or *"Something will turn up"*? Behind these thoughts is a belief that something will turn up to entertain you. In reality, however, happiness is the result of your taking responsibility, investing effort, being committed, and making things happen.

HOW TO THINK LESS RIGIDLY

Rigid thinking, often called "shouldism" or the "tyranny of the shoulds," involves a frequent use of the words "should," "must," and "ought to." The more you are inclined to use these words in your internal thinking or in your speech, the more pressure or stress you apply to yourself. The more "shoulds" and "oughts" you have weighing down on your shoulders, the more likely you are to feel frustration, anger, disappointment, guilt, and depression. These "shoulds" can usually be traced back to childhood and are often the internalized voice of our parents. The worst "should" is probably "I should be successful in everything I do." This puts you under an almost impossible burden.

There are three valid types of "should":
- UNIVERSAL SHOULD "If I drop an apple it should fall to the floor because of gravity."
- LEGAL SHOULD "I should not drive above the speed limit because it is breaking the law."
- MORAL SHOULD "I should not be rude to other people because I might upset them."

When you think, "I should clean the house," ask yourself what kind of "should" it is. It is clearly not a universal, legal, or moral should and, in fact, the word "should" is inappropriate here. What you really mean is that "I would like to…" or "There are advantages to cleaning the house." The more you keep the word "should" out of your thinking, the less stress you create for yourself.

BREAK THE TYRANNY OF THE "SHOULDS"

1 IDENTIFY "SHOULDS"
Write two lists. In your first list write down five "should" statements about how you think you should be, e.g. *"I should…"* In your second list write down five statements about how you believe others should be.

2 CHALLENGE
Take the most demanding "should" statement from each list and challenge it. Ask yourself, *"Where does this 'should' come from?"; "Who says I should?"; "Where is it written that I should?"; "Why should I?"*

3 WRITE DOWN THE PROS AND CONS
In two columns, list the advantages and disadvantages of a particular "should." Deliberately stretch your thinking, asking yourself, *"How does this help me? How does it hinder me?"*

4 SUBSTITUTE YOUR "SHOULDS"
Rewrite the statements on your lists, substituting a different phrase for "should." For example, instead of saying, *"He should be more outgoing,"* say, *"I would like it if he were more outgoing."*

5 "SHOULD" FILIBUSTER
Take five minutes out of every day to recite or write down all your "should," "must," and "ought to" statements. This will help you see how unhelpful, if not ridiculous, most of these statements are.

6 REDUCE "SHOULDS"
Count how many times you use the word "should" in a day. A wrist counter, as used by golfers, is useful for this exercise. Once you have a daily average, set targets to reduce the number and build in rewards and incentives.

LADDERING YOUR THOUGHTS

Confront your fears by asking yourself what is the worst thing that could happen.

"Thought laddering," sometimes called the "downward arrow technique" is a process where you identify and voice the worst fears you have about a situation. Some of these thoughts may be conscious, others you may be less aware of or may deliberately try not to think about. Most of us prefer not to think about our worst fears. The aim of this technique is to extract the chain of negative, distorted thoughts from the dark recesses of our minds so we can challenge them rationally in the clear light of day.

HOW TO BUILD A THOUGHT LADDER

Divide a piece of paper into two columns. In the left-hand column, write down a specific worry about the situation you fear. Then ask yourself, "What would be so bad about that?" and "What would happen then?" Write the answer below it and follow the downward arrow until you have unearthed all your worst fears. Now analyze each of your fears and write down a rational response in the right-hand column.

The benefits of this technique are that it makes you realize that your worst fears are often not as bad as you imagined. Second, it illustrates how irrational and distorted your thoughts can become if they are not rationally scrutinized. Third, it enables you to challenge your distorted, irrational thoughts and replace them with more rational ones.

A THOUGHT LADDER

IRRATIONAL THOUGHT	RATIONAL CHALLENGE
I'll panic on the plane – it will be terrible.	I'm catastrophizing. I'll feel anxious, but I've coped with that before. I now understand more about controlling anxiety.
I'll run down the aisle screaming, "I want to get out!"	Catastrophizing again. If I feel sick, I'll tell people how I am feeling.
There will be no help available. Just useless flight attendants, who know nothing about my fear of flying.	There is bound to be an experienced attendant. On a jet with 500 people there is sure to be at least one doctor.
I'll hyperventilate and lose control. They will have to physically overcome me to give me an injection.	I can control my breathing. If I need it, they might offer me a couple of tranquilizers to calm me down.
It will be so embarrassing. I'll never be able to live with myself.	What's wrong with being embarrassed? I'll never see any of these people again.
I'll be the only one on the plane with this kind of anxiety. I should cope better.	I'm personalizing. Out of 500 people, statistics suggest at least 50 will have anxiety problems.
It will ruin the vacation for my wife.	My wife is sympathetic. She understands me.
I'll never be able to go on vacation again.	That's black-and-white thinking. I'll go on vacation by car or train.

110

Positive self-statements

If you are going into a difficult situation that you know is likely to cause symptoms of anxiety, a useful way of coping is to prepare a ready-made menu of positive self-statements. These statements challenge and drive out potentially intrusive negative anxiety-provoking thoughts.

For example, if you have a fear of speaking in public and know you must make a speech as part of your preparation, identify and write down a list of positive statements that you can make before, during, and after the event. It helps to divide the stressful situation into three different phases – preparing, coping, and praising yourself afterward. Once you have prepared these statements you need to rehearse them repeatedly until you are familiar with them. In this way they can be called to mind when you need them, although it is sensible to carry a copy of your list with you into the anxiety-provoking situation. Modify this list to suit your personal situation.

Well-prepared self-statements help reduce anxiety.

Three simple steps for overcoming anxiety

1 Prepare beforehand

Go through this list of thoughts before you enter the anxiety-provoking situation.

- *It is not going to be as bad as I think.*
- *I am determined to get it right this time.*
- *It is better to go than not to go.*
- *Worry doesn't help.*
- *I will carry out my prepared exercises – I've been fully trained for this.*
- *I will monitor my breathing and stay in control.*
- *I will deal with negative thoughts by providing positive, rational alternatives.*

2 Cope during

These thoughts help when you are in the feared situation.

- *I'll take it slowly, step by step.*
- *I must concentrate on what I have to do.*
- *I'll use the word "relaxation" as a trigger to unwind.*
- *If I get tense I'll do some stomach breathing and some active relaxation of my muscles.*
- *These feelings are unpleasant but not harmful or dangerous*
- *I can tolerate anxiety; I've managed it many times before.*
- *The feelings always pass – what follows tension is relaxation.*
- *It is good to accept my anxiety.*

3 Praise afterward

These thoughts can help when you have gotten through the situation and coped with it.

- *Good work. That was quite a challenge.*
- *I managed to deal with that. I was not perfect, but it was an improvement.*
- *I handled that. It should be easier next time.*
- *I will write down how it really was so that I remember it next time.*
- *I'm improving.*

DEMOLISH YOUR WORRIES

Not everyone suffers from constant worrying, but for some, it is one of the biggest wasters of time and energy. It can put you through a great deal of suffering and stress. Most worrying is unnecessary, since the situations you fear rarely happen, and even if it is justified, worrying does not help. The only positive function of worrying is when it alerts you to danger and prompts action. If your car brakes feel strange or the red oil light comes on, it would be foolish to ignore these signals. However, if the red light's flashing spurs you to top off the oil, your reaction could be classed as problem-solving rather than worrying. Unlike worrying, problem-solving involves clearly identifying the problem, examining all available options, choosing the most advantageous, and then planning a strategy for accomplishing the chosen option.

Worrying is a natural enemy of good moods and damages physical and emotional health. It can make you depressed, cause panic attacks, lead you to smoke or drink, and cause sleep problems and physical symptoms, such as headaches and irritable bowel syndrome.

Worrying tends to make you introspective and self-centered. You develop a "selective attention," permanently searching for clues around you that confirm your worrying. If, for example, you worry that you are going to be robbed, you will notice "signs" that you would usually ignore. Worrying is also self-perpetuating – the more you worry, the worse you feel, the more you worry. If you are prone to worry, it helps to talk to other people. Their feedback often puts your thinking back into perspective and reduces the distortions, enabling you to air your feelings.

1 PINPOINT THE WORRYING THOUGHT

Worry is often the result of a number of half-formed thoughts chasing one another around in your conscious and sometimes unconscious mind. This vicious circle can be broken by deliberately "airing" or identifying the worrying thoughts. Write down your top five worries. Bringing these out into the open relieves pressure and gives you something to work on. Deal with one worry at a time.

2 LOOK FOR THE EVIDENCE

Instead of assuming that your thought is true, examine the evidence. What is the probability that it is true? Test out your thought by writing down the evidence for both sides of the argument. Rate the thought on a scale of 0 to 10 in terms of how much you actually believe it. For example, if you think "I am useless at this job," you might rate this as only 3 in terms of how much you believe the statement.

3 PUT YOURSELF IN SOMEONE ELSE'S SHOES

What alternative views are there? How would someone else view this situation? Think of two or three significant people in your life and imagine how they might view this situation. Put yourself in their shoes. What would they say to you? Talk to yourself out loud. What advice would they give?

4 COST-BENEFIT ANALYSIS

Question the effects of thinking the way you do. This question deals with your negative thoughts from the perspective of motivation rather than truth. Ask yourself, *"How will holding this thought help me and how will it hurt me?"* List the advantages and disadvantages of holding a particular negative thought. When the disadvantages are greater than the advantages, try to revise the thought.

5 THINK IN SHADES OF GRAY

Are you thinking in all-or-nothing, black-and-white terms? Do you see yourself as a total success or a total failure? This common style of distorted thinking misses out on the middle ground, the gray area between the black and white. Try to find the middle ground or a percentage between 0 and 100. For example, *"On this project I have been 60 percent successful."*

6 WATCH OUT FOR DISTORTED THINKING

Examine the list of types of distorted thinking on pp.106–107 and learn to prevent these type of thoughts. Ask yourself:
"Am I thinking in all-or-nothing terms?"; "Am I catastrophizing?"; "Am I personalizing?"; "Am I jumping to conclusions?"; "Am I focusing on the negative?"; "Am I living by fixed rules?"

7 EXPLORE THE WORST POSSIBLE OUTCOME

What is the worst thing that can happen? Imagine walking into a cave. You might be terrified. But if you switch on a flashlight your fear disappears as you see the limits of the cave. Our fantasies are usually much worse than a clearly identified worst option. By placing limits on our worries and identifying the worst possible outcome, they are easier to deal with.

8 BOX IN YOUR WORRIES

If you are plagued by worries, set aside 20 minutes per day that is dedicated worry time, in which you tackle each worry as a problem you need to solve. If you find yourself worrying at other times during the day, postpone that worry until the allotted time.

9 MAINTAIN PERSPECTIVE

Compare the present problem with other important issues in your life. For example, if you are worrying because you are stuck in a traffic jam and are going to be late for a meeting, how does this compare with the time when your mother was critically ill? People often say: *"It suddenly struck me that it's only a job... it's not the most important thing in my life."*

10 VISUALIZE YOURSELF IN TEN YEARS FROM NOW

Ask yourself if your worry will matter in ten years' time. Imagine that you are ten years older and are looking back to this time in your life. How important will this concern be in the long term? You will often find that, when observed from a distance, mountains can appear as molehills.

11 TURN WORRY INTO ACTION

Ask yourself what you can do to change or improve the situation. Make a list of the things you could do. Worry is only useful when it spurs you on to solve problems – although you can solve problems without the unpleasant side effects of worry. If constructive action is feasible and beneficial, then it is worth doing.

12 DISTRACT YOURSELF

If you reach the conclusion that there is nothing you can do, stop worrying and distract yourself with an absorbing activity. Distraction can work on a macro level, where you might change jobs or take up a hobby. Distraction can also work on a micro level, where you can take your mind off worrying thoughts by playing mental games, reciting poetry, or by focusing on a detail of your environment.

IMPROVING RELATIONSHIPS

Are you happy with your relationship? Do you wish the situation were different but feel powerless to bring about change? Rather than give up on it, discover the root of your problems and work it out with your partner.

Communication, love, and commitment are the vital ingredients for a successful long-term relationship.

Being in an intimate relationship can be a source of happiness, of stress, or an insulator against stress. Research indicates that people who are married or in a long-term relationship are physically and mentally healthier than single people, which gives rise to concern in societies where the divorce rate has been steadily increasing, or where young couples are rejecting traditional marriage commitments. Relationships are often abandoned because they "don't work," but this may be due to couples not knowing how to make them work.

One helpful theory suggests that long-term commitment can best be understood in terms of the following three main components:

■ INTIMACY This includes intimate communication, sharing possessions, giving and receiving emotional support, mutual understanding and respect, and a general state of happiness together

■ PASSION This includes all the elements associated with sexual attraction

■ COMMITMENT This is when you decide you love and want to stay with your partner.

If your relationship has all three components it is one of consummate love. Romantic love has two out of the three components – intimacy and passion, without commitment, and a platonic relationship has intimacy without passion or commitment.

At the heart of all good relationships is a balance of exchange in which each partner gives and receives. If one partner gives a lot but receives little in return, he or she is likely to feel dissatisfied. This "give and take" requires a number of key skills. You must be aware of your own needs and express what you want and how you feel, and you must listen to and understand the needs of your partner. You must also be able to accept each other's differences and have realistic beliefs. Unrealistic beliefs may lead to unrealistic demands and, ultimately, to the break-up of the relationship.

TOP TEN FACTORS THAT MAKE A RELATIONSHIP WORK

1 Faithfulness and loyalty to partner

2 Mutual respect and appreciation

3 Understanding and tolerance

4 Not wanting to change partner

5 Fulfilling sexual relationship

6 Talking openly and communicating

7 Sharing common interests

8 Expressing emotions

9 Sharing chores

10 Having independent interests

ARE YOU SATISFIED WITH YOUR RELATIONSHIP?

This questionnaire looks at the ingredients of an ideal "strong" relationship and is designed to help you identify areas to work on. Answer the following questions and calculate your score.

SCORING
Agree 2 • Partly agree 1 • Disagree 0

1 We both like doing similar things.

2 I enjoy talking with my partner.

3 We can have fun and laugh together.

4 My partner makes me feel loved.

5 My partner talks to me about how he/she is feeling.

6 My partner is sensitive and aware of my needs.

7 I trust my partner.

8 Our relationship continually evolves.

9 My partner respects me and what I do.

10 After a disagreement we can "agree to disagree."

11 We have a good sexual relationship.

12 I express both positive and negative feelings to my partner.

13 I show affection to my partner.

14 When conflicts arise they are resolved quite quickly.

15 I am happy with our relationship.

16 I am committed to our relationship.

17 I accept my partner and do not expect him/her to change.

18 It always helps to sit down and talk things through.

19 I think I am aware of my partner's needs and likes.

20 I feel emotionally close to my partner.

TOTAL SCORE

INTERPRETATION

Over 30 High rating
You appear to have all the ingredients of a good, strong relationship.

18–30 Medium rating
You appear to have many of the ingredients of a good relationship, but there is room for improvement.

Below 18 Low rating
Your relationship appears to lack a number of vital ingredients. Read the following section carefully.

This questionnaire is intended as a starting point for you and your partner to enable you to examine areas of your relationship that could be improved. Bear in mind, however, that if you want your relationship to work, both you and your partner will need to work at it. Accept that your partner is different from you and respect these differences. Remember, he or she is not telepathic, so you need to make sure you communicate your needs and feelings. Do not expect your partner to provide you with everything you need. For useful advice turn to the pages in this section IMPROVING RELATIONSHIPS *pp.114–125*. You will also find helpful information in ASSERTIVENESS *pp.82–93* and SELF-CARE *pp.126–139*, particularly DEVELOPING HOBBIES AND INTERESTS *p.136* and EXPANDING YOUR CIRCLE OF FRIENDS *p.137*.

COMMUNICATING IN RELATIONSHIPS

The key to a sound and longlasting relationship is communication. If you are to develop deep, strong relationships, you need to be able to share information about yourself and encourage your partner similarly to express him- or herself. Good communication, with a natural flow, consists of three essential skills: listening to what the other person is saying; expressing how you feel and what you think; and accepting the other person's opinions and feelings, even if they are different from your own. Behavioral scientists have identified particular ways in which some people communicate with each other that may permanently damage their relationship. These "communication spoilers" interrupt the speaker's natural flow, making him or her less inclined to talk. They occur most commonly in times of stress, but if they are allowed to continue over a prolonged period, they cause conversation to suffer, resentment to build up, and emotional distance to increase.

For the average person, listening takes up more waking hours than any other activity. Sadly, few people are good listeners. Research suggests that three-quarters of all oral

COMMUNICATION SPOILERS

- Judging, blaming, criticizing
- Name calling, putting people down
- Moralizing, ordering people around
- Offering solutions and solving problems rather than listening
- Excessive inappropriate questioning using closed questions
- Interrupting, finishing sentences
- Dismissing the other person's concerns

BE A GOOD LISTENER

1 FACE THE SPEAKER Sit where you can clearly see the speaker's face, on the same level. Make eye contact but do not stare.

2 USE OPEN QUESTIONS Do not allow one-word answers. Allow the speaker to open up. Say *"How did you feel?"* and not *"Did you feel sad?"*

3 BE ENCOURAGING Put the speaker at ease by making encouraging noises to show you are listening. Say *"Yes,"* *"Hmm,"* *"Really?"* Nod your head.

4 PARAPHRASE Briefly restate the essence of what has been said in your own words. For example, *"Your son is really growing up, then..."*

5 DO NOT INTERRUPT Allow the speaker to think and express his or her feelings without interruptions or prompting. Wait. Be patient.

6 REFLECT Mirror back to the speaker the emotions and meanings in what he or she says. For example, *"So you're saying that you're angry with me."*

communication is ignored, misinterpreted, or simply forgotten. It is enormously frustrating to talk to somebody about something important and find that they have not really listened but are responding in an automatic, preprogrammed, mechanical way. Listening is more than just hearing. Effective listening is an active, not a passive, skill, made up of a number of set components. The quality of your listening greatly affects the nature of the speaker's communication and your ability to understand what has been said. Listening skills affect your personal relationships.

Relationships are at their healthiest when both parties can express themselves assertively and openly. Disclosing personal information helps your relationship develop – but this needs to be done in a particular way, and in a gradual and reciprocal fashion. Remember, you and your partner are different people. You cannot always agree on the way you think and feel. Accepting how your partner is and tolerating the differences, and any resulting frustration, is an essential key for relationships to flourish. Although personality is clearly a factor in the way you relate to others, it has been suggested that men and women are fundamentally different in the way they communicate. This may be due to the process of socialization, as men are programmed to be more competitive, or it may be a genetic trait.

- Men tend to offer solutions to problems and want to achieve results, while women tend to share feelings and discuss difficulties.
- Men's talk tends to revolve around passing on information and displaying knowledge, skill, status, and independence, while women's talk is based on sharing similar experiences, creating intimacy and rapport.
- Men are more prone to mull things over, then formulate and express the most correct, practical, and useful response, whereas women are more prone to thinking aloud, sharing their inner dialogue, often using poetic license to make their feelings known.

Being aware of and tolerating some of these differences in communication styles can lead to a more accepting attitude to your partner.

EXPRESS YOURSELF

1 TIME IT RIGHT
Choose the right time and place. Avoid discussing important issues when you are tired. It may help to make notes beforehand.

2 BE CONCISE
Stick to the point. Do not trawl through old, stale issues. Do not allow yourself to nag or be sidetracked

3 TAKE RESPONSIBILITY
Begin with "I" to show that you accept responsibility. Say *"I feel..."* or *"I think..."* and not *"You make me feel..."*

4 BE ASSERTIVE
Describe irritating behavior, your feelings, and the effects. Say, *"When you won't get up, I feel annoyed, because it makes me late."*

5 CHOOSE YOUR WORDS
Be careful not to insult, threaten, or denigrate. Be honest and positive, but tactful. Criticize actions rather than personality.

6 SEEK A REACTION
Make your point and then listen to the other person's point of view. Understand and accept his or her reaction.

HOW YOUR PAST AFFECTS THE PRESENT

We all bring to any new relationship the baggage of past relationships – the patterns of behavior, the feelings, and the expectations. A helpful way of understanding how your personality is shaped is to imagine it as comprising three voices or states, of parent, adult, and child. The parent part is the internalized voices of your own parents, or authority figures, offering advice, judging, caring, supporting, and controlling. This parent state can be divided into the critical parent and the supportive parent. The voice of the child is your own voice when you were a child, with all the strong feelings and responses that were laid down early in your life – the tempers, fun, laughter, creativity, rebelliousness, and attention-seeking. This child state can also be broken down into two

OUR CHILD, ADULT, AND PARENTAL VOICES

The first relationships you have with your parents and family members have the most influence and set patterns of behavior that can stay with you through life. Our personalities have three different states: parent, child, *and adult. In a healthy relationship, partners communicate on all levels. However, if you or your partner stays in either parent or child mode, problems may follow.*

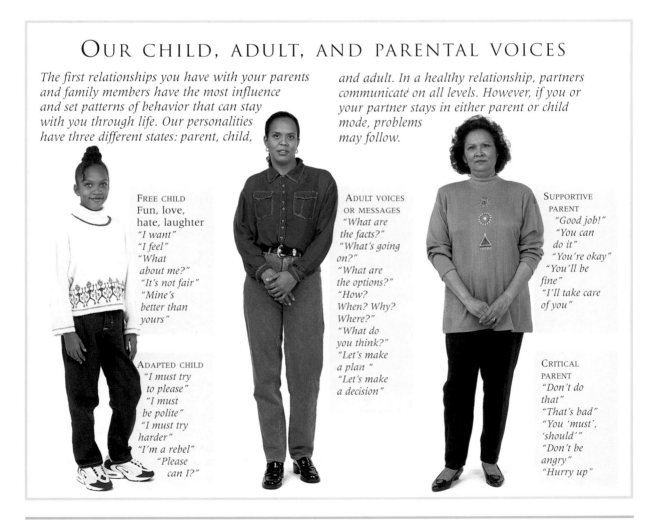

FREE CHILD
Fun, love, hate, laughter
"I want"
"I feel"
"What about me?"
"It's not fair"
"Mine's better than yours"

ADAPTED CHILD
"I must try to please"
"I must be polite"
"I must try harder"
"I'm a rebel"
"Please can I?"

ADULT VOICES OR MESSAGES
"What are the facts?"
"What's going on?"
"What are the options?"
"How? When? Why? Where?"
"What do you think?"
"Let's make a plan "
"Let's make a decision"

SUPPORTIVE PARENT
"Good job!"
"You can do it"
"You're okay"
"You'll be fine"
"I'll take care of you"

CRITICAL PARENT
"Don't do that"
"That's bad"
"You 'must', should'"
"Don't be angry"
"Hurry up"

aspects; the free, spontaneous child, and the adapted child, who is reacting to the adult world. In between these two powerful parent and child voices is your own adult voice, which has developed as a result of your personal experiences of the world. This adult voice or state is the rational, objective, decision-making aspect of your personality.

In any relationship it is helpful to be able to move between all three voices. In a healthy relationship, partners communicate with each other as adult to adult, parent to child, child to parent, and child to child. However, if one partner is always in parent state, it tends to push the other partner into child state. We move in and out of these different states, and, at any one time, one of these states will exert most influence. The adult voice, is, however, the executive and needs to be able to control the other two voices.

Depending on the situation, certain states are more appropriate than others. For example, the adult is more appropriate for making decisions at work, while the free child might be more appropriate for having fun at a party, and the parental state might be best for looking after your partner if he or she is ill.

To communicate effectively with others, you need to be in a state that complements the state of the other person. For example, if you are communicating in adult-to-adult mode and say to your partner, "I've bought a new sweater, what do you think?," the expectation is that your partner will give an adult response. However, if he or she responds as a critical parent to a child and says, "That's ridiculous. What a waste of money. You know we can't afford it," you are likely to feel as if you are being told off, like a naughty child, and may feel unhappy. This type of interaction is not complementary; you are not on the same wavelength, and the result is likely to be anxiety.

Problems may arise if you are not aware of the voices in your past.

CHANGE THE PATTERNS

1 UNDERSTAND THE PROCESS

If you can trace your adult, child, and parent voices and messages back, and appraise them with the adult part of your personality, you can free yourself from their influence. Recognize that your partner has his or her own different voices and so there is no point in blaming him or her.

2 IDENTIFY THE MESSAGE

Make a list of messages that were handed down to you from the past: for example, *"It is bad to show anger"* or *"Don't cry."* Link these messages to your way of dealing with or reacting to these emotions now. Reappraise the message. Is it now redundant, or could it be modified or retained? Make this a conscious decision.

3 RECOGNIZE TRIGGERS

Be aware that small events may produce disproportionate emotional reactions. For example, you may feel devastated and unbearably rejected if your partner is angry with you. This may be because, as a child, your family deemed anger unacceptable, while for your partner, the expression of anger was a healthy part of childhood.

EXERCISES TO ENHANCE YOUR RELATIONSHIP

Every relationship is likely to suffer if either partner is under stress, whatever the cause. Too many demands can make it all too easy to neglect your relationship, often causing problems with communication, loss of sex drive, or simply taking your partner for granted.

Unless you can step back and rectify the situation, your deteriorating relationship will cause further stress until the situation comes to a head and fundamental damage is done. The following exercises have been chosen to allow you and your partner to work on developing skills that form the ingredients of a sound relationship. Take some time together to go through

each of these and learn to appreciate each other. However good your relationship, there are always areas that can be spiced up, enhanced, and worked on. These exercises will teach you to understand the importance of accepting differences in each other and of communicating feelings. You must be prepared to change aspects of your behavior that your partner does not like, to be more spontaneous, and to spend spare time together. If you have neglected the habit of showing appreciation, you may need a jolt. It is often the little things in a relationship that are most important; you may need to be reminded of them.

1 PINPOINT SIMILARITIES AND DIFFERENCES

On a large sheet of paper, list all the ways that you and your partner are alike, and all the ways that you are different. Include interests, attitudes, skills, likes, dislikes, personalities, and general outlook. Do the exercise separately, and then discuss what you have written. Talk about the aspects in which you are alike, enjoy the feelings of similarity, and add to each other's list. Now discuss areas in which you feel you are different. Identify differences that you are happy with and would like to continue, and differences that you find hard to accept and would like the other person to change.

2 MAKE A CONTRACT

Draw up a list of the specific behaviors that you would like your partner to increase, or do more of, and the specific behaviors you would like your partner to decrease or do less of. Then agree to exchange a behavior, of equal difficulty, and agree to make a contract. For example, *"I will put the top on the toothpaste every day, and you will hang up your towel."* It is best to start on small, simple tasks that are relatively easy to achieve and gradually work up to more difficult tasks.

3 REDISCOVER SPONTANEITY

After a while couples know each other so well that routines become predictable. Make a deliberate effort to do things differently, and break old familiar habits. For example, sleep on the other side of the bed, dress differently, sit in a different chair to watch television, get up very early, tell a joke, miss a meal. One variation on this exercise is to make a pact with your partner for a week to each do something slightly differently every day. At the end of each day you and your partner have to guess what the spontaneous thing was.

4 MAKE A DATE

Coordinate your schedules and make a deliberate effort to spend some special time alone together each week. This should not be watching television but perhaps having a leisurely meal together, or sitting and talking over a drink. Once a month make one of these dates together a special occasion, when you go out to see a show, to a restaurant, or do another activity that you both enjoy. Take turns choosing where to go and organizing a babysitter for the evening.

5 DO YOU RECEIVE THE APPRECIATION YOU DESERVE?

This is a useful exercise to help you learn where and how to support, develop, and please each other. For a relationship to flourish, each partner needs to give and receive small signs, or "strokes," of appropriate appreciation. List all the things that you do, at home or at work, for which you think you deserve strokes. Then go through the list and put a plus sign next to items where you feel you receive sufficient strokes, and a minus next to the items where you feel you receive insufficient strokes. Do this separately and then exchange and discuss lists.

6 TREAT EACH OTHER

Make an agreement to take turns, each day, to ask your partner to do something for you or with you that you will enjoy. This should be a simple favor that your partner can do without feeling uncomfortable. Tasks might include watching a television program together, cooking you a meal, washing your hair for you, giving a massage, going for a walk, making you a drink, or sitting down and talking for ten minutes. Sometimes couples find it very difficult to think of favors that they would like since they have lost the habit of being together and helping each other. Take time to think about it and start with something small.

7 LITTLE THINGS ARE IMPORTANT

Look down the following checklist of simple relationship-enhancing tasks and check off the ones that you do regularly.

1 Kiss or touch when saying good bye.
2 Bring surprise gifts: flowers or candy.
3 Ask about and discuss the day your partner has had.
4 Plan a night out in advance.
5 Compliment your partner on his or her appearance.
6 Cuddle and be affectionate without sex.
7 Touch hands when talking or walking.
8 Make your partner a drink.
9 Surprise your partner with a love note or a poem.
10 Create "quality" time alone together.

8 WRITE A STRUCTURED LETTER

If you're feeling angry or frustrated with each other, instead of having a fight, each write a letter expressing your feelings under the following seven headings:

- "I feel angry that…"
- "I feel sad that…"
- "I feel afraid that…"
- "I regret that…"
- "I love it when…"
- "I would like it if…"
- "I am sorry…"

Write a few sentences about each feeling, then exchange letters and discuss your letters with your partner.

9 OPEN TALK

Set aside a period of time when each partner has the opportunity to talk openly and the other partner has to listen without comment or interruption. Agree on a set period between 5 and 25 minutes each. If one partner finds it difficult to talk, start with the shorter time period. Then decide who is going to go first. The first person then says whatever is on his or her mind and how he or she is feeling. The other person listens without interrupting or commenting. Then change roles. This can be a difficult but rewarding exercise, particularly if you are having trouble communicating. Make an agreement that either partner can ask for an open talk at any time.

MISPLACED JEALOUSY

Feelings of misplaced jealousy, which are not based on a specific cause, can make us behave in ways that can destroy relationships. Jealousy is caused by a number of fears that often have their roots in childhood.

■ FEAR OF LOSING SOMETHING IMPORTANT Jealous people are often insecure, lack self-confidence, and have difficulty believing that somebody else can love them for themselves. This may stem from a childhood feeling of never having been unconditionally loved. All feelings of self-worth subsequently tend to be based on possessions, personal or professional achievements, or physical attractiveness.

■ FEAR OF CHANGE The subconscious irrational thought here is that change is always for the worst. This may stem from a childhood in which change, adventure, or spontaneity were discouraged, usually by overprotective parents.

■ FEAR OF BEING ALONE If you felt abandoned as a child, you may fear being alone and mistrust others.

Relationships in which either one or both of the partners is possessively jealous often have a number of unhealthy characteristics:

■ Master/slave mentality, where one partner regards the other as a possession or something owned rather than as a free individual.

■ A naive notion that people in a relationship should love each other unconditionally, irrespective of their behavior toward each other, however unreasonable this may be.

■ A lack of awareness as to how jealous behavior makes the other person feel.

Understand why you feel jealous.

COPING WITH MISPLACED JEALOUSY

1 ACCEPT RESPONSIBILITY
It is no use continuously blaming your partner. Nobody else can make you jealous – you do it yourself by the way you think.

2 EXAMINE YOUR FEELINGS
Connect the past with the present and try to discover the roots of your feelings. What is this emotional overreaction about?

3 RESTRICT YOUR BEHAVIOR
If you must display jealousy, agree to show it for a period of, say, 20 minutes only. Encourage your partner to be tough and not to tolerate an inquisition.

4 BE INDEPENDENT AND CONFIDENT
Take up a hobby that does not involve your partner. Learn to trust rather than control. Build up your self-esteem. List reasons why your partner likes you.

5 CHALLENGE IRRATIONAL THINKING
Fight thoughts, such as *"He really likes Linda, he prefers her to me, he's going to have an affair with her."* This is "all-or-nothing thinking" and "catastrophizing."

6 IMAGINE LIFE WITHOUT JEALOUSY
Would this solve all your relationship problems? Does your jealousy serve as a focus for worrying, which detracts from other underlying problems?

SULKING

Sulking is an unhelpful way of showing anger or disappointment. Being silent, unwilling to talk, and freezing another person out do not communicate what he or she is supposed to have done, therefore, progress cannot be made. Sulky behavior often has its roots in childhood, when parents may have avoided expressing negative feelings, not permitting the child to show anger openly.

If you are prone to sulking, it is likely that you have the following thinking habits:
■ You might be inclined to interpreting feelings and thoughts as facts without really testing them out, or only testing them out in a halfhearted manner. You might think, "I thought it, therefore it must be true."
■ You are likely to be prone to demanding, fixed rules, and "shouldism"-type thinking. For example, you may think that your partner "should" behave differently or that the world "should" be a fairer place.

■ You are also likely to have a tendency to "awfulize," believing that if you are being treated unfairly, it is awful and you can't bear it, and you are helpless to change anything. You feel self-pity – "Oh, poor me."

We only sulk with people we feel close to emotionally, usually because they have done something we do not like or because they have not done something we wanted them to do. Sulking is only effective if the other person is in close proximity to witness our suffering. The functions of sulking are: to punish the other person; to achieve what we want; to extract proof of caring; to protect ourselves from pain; and to restore power.

If you live with someone who sulks, you need to be patient and appreciate that he or she has difficulty asserting themselves. Ask the person, when not sulking, how you can help when he or she is sulking. Do not reinforce sulky behavior or give in to it.

STOP YOURSELF SULKING

1 LOOK AT ADVANTAGES AND DISADVANTAGES
Sulking might make you feel in control, but the disadvantage is that it does not resolve problems.

2 UNDERSTAND WHY YOU SULK
As a child, were you allowed to express negative feelings of anger? Was it okay to be assertive?

3 ANALYZE A RECENT EPISODE OF SULKING
Think of a recent sulk. Identify your most prominent feeling. Did you feel criticized or rejected?

4 EXPRESS HOW YOU FELT
Put into words your interpretation of what happened and how you felt. It may help to write it down.

5 LOOK OUT FOR DISTORTED THINKING
Watch out for unhelpful thinking patterns, e.g., "awfulizing" and using "should" and "ought to."

6 EXPRESS YOUR NEGATIVE FEELINGS
State why you sulked, what you want, and express how you feel (see pp.88–89).

IMPROVING YOUR SEX LIFE

There is no such thing as a normal sexual relationship; but we can talk in terms of a satisfactory sexual relationship, where both partners feel mutually satisfied. To have and maintain a fulfilling long-term sexual relationship can help cement relationships, reflect intimacy, and ultimately relieve stress. A successful long-lasting sexual relationship is invariably tied to other aspects of the relationship, and it is unwise to separate sex from the rest of the relationship.

If you are stressed, depressed, or simply just very tired and run down, the loss of sexual interest (libido) can often be a prominent symptom. If unchecked, this may lead to secondary relationship problems, such as a lack of intimacy or guilt, frustration, anger, and resentment from your partner, which further add to your stresses. It is important, therefore, when stressed,

to make an effort to maintain intimacy, good communication, and affectionate contact with your partner outside the bedroom, so that sexual intimacy within the bedroom has a better chance of surviving.

Having a relaxed attitude toward sex is an important starting point for a satisfactory sexual relationship. Research suggests that sensitivity, the right feelings, and intimacy are often more important than orgasm, especially for women. Give yourself permission for sex to be enjoyable and for you to express yourself. Inhibitions and rigid thinking about what you should or should not do can often be traced back to childhood and the messages that your parents, authority figures, and peers gave you. If these messages are restrictive, they need to be challenged and thrown out. Follow the pleasure of your body and treat it as an adventure.

1 CHOOSE THE RIGHT PARTNER

A good sexual relationship is more difficult to maintain if you do not feel attracted to and aroused by your partner. It is hard to pinpoint sexual chemistry, but most people intuitively know whether or not they feel sexually attracted to someone. Given a background of mutual attraction, affection, honesty, and trust, sexual fulfillment is possible.

2 ACCEPT THAT SEXUAL FEELINGS CHANGE

With time, the intensity of early passion is likely to fade as sex gradually plays a less prominent part in your relationship. However, you can compensate for the loss of these early, intense feelings by developing a comfortable, trusting, relationship, where you both know what pleases each other. Levels of sexual interest also decrease with hormonal changes during and after pregnancy and in times of stress.

3 KEEP COMMUNICATING

Talk about sex, your likes and dislikes, and different needs. A man may have a greater appetite for sex and be more concerned about erections and orgasms, while a woman may be more concerned about intimacy. These differences need to be discussed and compromises worked out. If you are not in the mood for lovemaking, learn to say no and reject the invitation without rejecting the person.

4 EDUCATE YOURSELF ABOUT SEX

Read a book or manual about lovemaking. Information about the mechanisms of arousal, the need for foreplay, and the physical changes during lovemaking are essential for good sex.

5 LIKE YOUR BODY

Examine yourself in front of a mirror. Think of the parts of your body that you like and try to feel affection for the parts you are unhappy about. Look at and explore your genitals, and touch yourself. If you can feel comfortable exploring your body, it becomes easier to allow your lover to do the same.

6 LEARN WHAT GIVES YOU PLEASURE

By touching and caressing yourself, you can find out what kind of stimulation you like best. Masturbation is an extension of this and is not physically or mentally harmful, nor does it matter how often you do it. The vast majority of men and women masturbate, although many suffer from irrational guilt.

7 DISCOVER WHAT YOU LIKE BEST TOGETHER

What turns you on will not necessarily do the same for your partner. Experiment with different ways of making love and pleasing each other. Talk while you are making love, trying to be specific in your encouragement or discouragement. For example, you might say, *"That's pleasant, I like you doing that"* or *"I'd rather you didn't touch me there, it tickles."*

8 OVERCOME INHIBITION

If you feel inhibited, reexamine your attitudes that sex is "sinful," "dirty," "should not be discussed," or that it "should not be enjoyed." Develop your fantasies by looking at books, magazines, or videos. Your imagination is a safe place to let your inhibitions go, and experiment with new feelings. Practice losing control during lovemaking: breathe more heavily or moan more loudly.

9 BE SELFISH AND GENEROUS

Lovemaking is a mixture of selfishness and generosity. Selfishness means asking for what you want and taking what you need. Generosity means concentrating on pleasing your partner and giving what he or she wants. Take active responsibility for your own orgasm by showing your partner what you like and where to touch you, or touch yourself.

10 MAKE TIME

In the early days of a relationship, you make time for lovemaking. You need to continue to do this if you want your sex life to remain fulfilling. Go to bed early and make time for sex, so that it is not just fitted in at the end of the day when you are tired. Creating the right atmosphere requires effort. Do not rush lovemaking; spend time touching, gradually increasing pleasure, before building up to intercourse.

11 INTRODUCE VARIETY – INJECT SOME FUN

Break out of your routine by introducing variety. Make love somewhere different, other than a bed, make love at an unusual time, vary positions, vary who initiates, or read an erotic magazine or book together. Massage each other with scented oils, or have a bath or a shower together.

12 BE FLEXIBLE

A fulfilling sex life means recognizing the need for flexibility and changeability. Just as our appetite for food varies, so does our appetite for sex. Accept that occasionally we may want a sexual three-course meal, while at other times we may want just a quick snack.

SELF-CARE

If you keep yourself fit, healthy, and relaxed, you are better prepared emotionally and physically to tackle the stresses of everyday life. Find out how well you look after yourself – and discover why self-care is necessary.

If you look after yourself, you feel good and are better able to care for others who depend on you.

We all need to take care of ourselves. This means relaxing, eating a healthy diet, exercising, having fun, involving ourselves in absorbing activities, taking breaks, being with family and friends, and maintaining a balance between work and play.

One of the best strategies for improving mental fitness and warding off harmful stress is to give yourself treats or rewards. These provide enjoyment and pleasure and make you feel good, as well as providing you with a purpose, motivation, and contrast to everyday chores. If you do not build in rewards, and tasks are done out of a sense of duty, you risk becoming burned out. A treat may be simply sitting down for ten minutes with a hot drink and the newspaper, or a longer-term reward such as a vacation after a period of hard work.

WHY YOU NEED TO BE SELFISH

The word "selfish" has a negative connotation for most people. However, before you can give other people what they need, it is important that you are first able to take care of yourself. Some people find this difficult and sense guilt, due to an underlying belief that caring for themselves is somehow self-indulgent or wrong. As a reaction, these people often become "selfless," spending all their time putting others' wants and needs first. Overburdening yourself in this way for the sake of others, and becoming a martyr, saying, "Don't worry, I can manage," when you really need help, has a negative effect on all involved. Not only do you cause resentment to build up and create stress, which may eventually burst out in anger or push you into depression – but you also make other people feel guilty. This can be an undeclared and manipulative way of punishing others that may damage relationships in the long term.

Very often, this style of behavior is learned from parents or is the result of low self-esteem. Parental messages such as, "Always put others first" and "Gimme never gets," subtly instill in the child listener a non-assertive attitude toward self-care.

LAUGHTER

Sometimes the demands of everyday life make you forget to have fun and laugh as you did when you were a child. Research shows that children laugh about 150 times a day, while adults laugh only six. As well as improving respiration, lowering blood pressure, and tuning up the heart muscles, laughter boosts the immune system, making you healthier and protecting you from illness and disease.

Laughing can help you stay healthy.

HOW WELL DO YOU TAKE CARE OF YOURSELF?

*Self-care encompasses attending to your physical, mental, emotional, and social needs.
It means managing your time and being assertive in prioritizing for yourself. Only when you can care
for yourself can you care for others. Answer the questions to see how well you take care of yourself.*

SCORING
Very like me 4 • Like me 3 • Unlike me 2 • Very unlike me 1

1 I occasionally give myself something pleasant like a present or a treat.

2 I make time for relaxing activities.

3 I believe I have to be selfish at times.

4 I like it when others take care of me when I am ill.

5 I plan special events, such as vacations and outings, that I can look forward to.

6 Every day I make sure I have some time to do something pleasurable for my own enjoyment.

7 I make a point of taking care of my appearance and health.

8 I can say no when people make demands on me.

9 I praise myself when I do a good job.

10 I avoid drinking too much alcohol.

11 I deliberately exercise and keep fit.

12 I consciously make time to cultivate friendships with people I like.

13 I make a point of eating healthy food and do not skip meals.

14 I make time to engage in absorbing meaningful hobbies and activities.

15 Sometimes I have to put my own needs first even if I hurt others.

16 I feel other people are responsible for solving their own problems.

17 I pace myself rather than going flat out all the time.

18 I feel in control of my life and do not live according to other people's wishes.

19 I avoid taking harmful drugs such as tobacco.

20 I am able to acknowledge and discuss my good points.

TOTAL SCORE

INTERPRETATION

Over 54 Higher than average
You have a good sense of self-care and take care of yourself well.

40–54 Average
You take care of yourself quite well – but you could improve.

Below 40 Poor
Your life is not your own. You need to learn to take care of yourself.

A low total score may indicate that you have problems with guilt and poor assertiveness. You should read carefully through this section on SELF-CARE *pp.126–139*, then go back to ASSERTIVENESS *pp.82–93*, COMMON IRRATIONAL BELIEFS *p.110*, and HOW TO THINK LESS RIGIDLY *p.111*.

LEARNING TO RELAX

When you are stressed your body goes into a state of high physical arousal. Your body systems speed up, your muscles tense, your heart beats more quickly, and your breathing becomes quicker and shallower. This reaction, or "flight or fight" response, produces secondary symptoms such as headache, backache, tightness in the chest, dizziness, sweating, and tiredness, which produce more worry, which produces more tension, creating a spiralling vicious circle. If you can deliberately train yourself to break this chain of events and reverse the process by relaxing your body and slowing down, you can turn off tension. If you find yourself tensing up,

making a fist, hunching your shoulders, or sitting on the edge of your chair, then adopt a comfortable posture, concentrate on your breathing, and deliberately relax your body. Plan your day so you have regular breaks and enough time to complete tasks without rushing. Introduce pleasure and treats into your day – the more you enjoy yourself, the more relaxed you will feel.

Teaching yourself to relax is an active skill that has to be learned and requires practice. Research shows that relaxation training reduces symptoms of anxiety and stress, and decreases the incidence of illnesses such as high blood pressure and heart disease.

THREE-MINUTE RELAXATION ROUTINE

This brief relaxation routine should only take two to three minutes and is useful if you suddenly find yourself in the middle of a stressful situation. It helps if you already know the longer Progressive

Muscle-relaxation Routine (opposite). Tune in to your breathing and choose an instruction such as "Let go" or "Calm." Repeat this word or phrase in your mind as you relax. This is your cue to relax.

1 Concentrate on relaxing using your cue word. Tune in to your breathing and take in one deep breath and hold it.

2 While you are holding your breath, tense up a group of muscles, such as the muscles in your face, legs, or arms.

3 As you breathe out, relax the tensed muscles and let go. Feel all your tension slip away. Drop your shoulders sideways.

PROGRESSIVE MUSCLE-RELAXATION TECHNIQUE

This relaxation exercise involves tightening each muscle group in your body, holding for 5 seconds, and then gradually releasing and relaxing for 10–15 seconds. It takes about 20 minutes to perform, and can bring tremendous benefits if you fit it into your daily routine.

1 Sit or lie down quietly in a comfortable position, with no distractions or possibilities of interruption. Begin by thinking slow, relaxing thoughts. Bring to mind any comfortable image you can imagine, such as lying by a stream in a beautiful forest. Take three deep breaths and focus on the tension in your body.

2 Go through each of the muscle groups in the suggested order, beginning with the hands and then working up the body and back down to the feet. With practice you will soon be familiar with the sequence. Tense the muscles as tightly as you can. Hold for 5 seconds and then gradually release.

3 As you release the muscles, relax and feel the tension drain away. Imagine the blood circulating in the different muscle groups. Concentrate on the feelings in the muscles as they go from tight to loose. Notice the difference between tension and relaxation. Perform the tightening and relaxing of each muscle group twice before moving on.

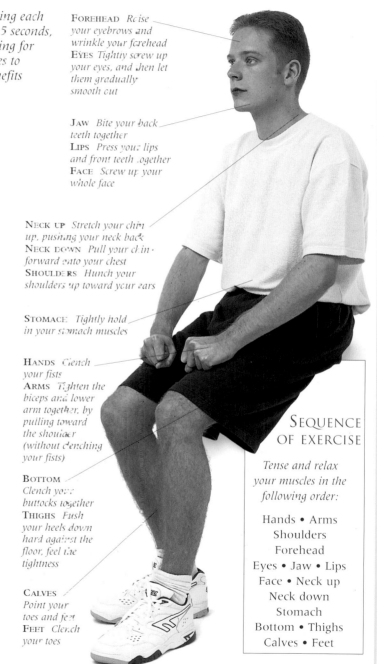

FOREHEAD *Raise your eyebrows and wrinkle your forehead*
EYES *Tightly screw up your eyes, and then let them gradually smooth out*

JAW *Bite your back teeth together*
LIPS *Press your lips and front teeth together*
FACE *Screw up your whole face*

NECK UP *Stretch your chin up, pushing your neck back*
NECK DOWN *Pull your chin forward onto your chest*
SHOULDERS *Hunch your shoulders up toward your ears*

STOMACH *Tightly hold in your stomach muscles*

HANDS *Clench your fists*
ARMS *Tighten the biceps and lower arm together, by pulling toward the shoulder (without clenching your fists)*

BOTTOM *Clench your buttocks together*
THIGHS *Push your heels down hard against the floor, feel the tightness*

CALVES *Point your toes and feet*
FEET *Clench your toes*

SEQUENCE OF EXERCISE

Tense and relax your muscles in the following order:

Hands • Arms
Shoulders
Forehead
Eyes • Jaw • Lips
Face • Neck up
Neck down
Stomach
Bottom • Thighs
Calves • Feet

RELAXED BREATHING

Your breathing patterns reflect your state of mind and emotions. When you are stressed or anxious you tend toward thoracic breathing, or rapid shallow breathing from high in the chest, with frequent sighs. The most relaxed breathing is slow, stomach-centered breathing from the diaphragm, a domelike muscle between the chest and the abdominal cavity. The way you breathe is also affected by posture. If you you lean forward and your chest and rib cage are concave, the diaphragm is immobilized and breathing is confined to the upper chest area. Thoracic breathing causes the body to eliminate too much carbon dioxide, which makes the blood too alkaline. As a result, the blood vessels in the brain narrow, slowing the circulation of oxygen and producing unpleasant side effects such as tingling sensations, palpitations, dizziness, chest pains, and feelings of faintness. This process is called hyperventilation (see p.20). Learn how to recognize thoracic breathing.

BREATHING AWARENESS EXERCISE

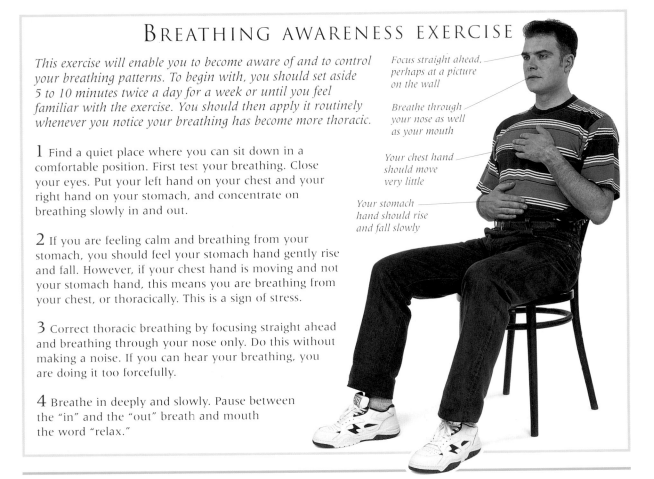

This exercise will enable you to become aware of and to control your breathing patterns. To begin with, you should set aside 5 to 10 minutes twice a day for a week or until you feel familiar with the exercise. You should then apply it routinely whenever you notice your breathing has become more thoracic.

1 Find a quiet place where you can sit down in a comfortable position. First test your breathing. Close your eyes. Put your left hand on your chest and your right hand on your stomach, and concentrate on breathing slowly in and out.

2 If you are feeling calm and breathing from your stomach, you should feel your stomach hand gently rise and fall. However, if your chest hand is moving and not your stomach hand, this means you are breathing from your chest, or thoracically. This is a sign of stress.

3 Correct thoracic breathing by focusing straight ahead and breathing through your nose only. Do this without making a noise. If you can hear your breathing, you are doing it too forcefully.

4 Breathe in deeply and slowly. Pause between the "in" and the "out" breath and mouth the word "relax."

Focus straight ahead, perhaps at a picture on the wall

Breathe through your nose as well as your mouth

Your chest hand should move very little

Your stomach hand should rise and fall slowly

REDUCING ENVIRONMENTAL STRESS

A lack of sunlight can cause stress and depression.

Colors can affect your feelings and moods.

Your environment can have a noticeable effect on your state of well-being and your ability to cope with stress. Noise, light, air quality, space, and color can all exert an influence on your mood.

Most people feel happier and healthier in bright sunlight. Scientists have shown that natural light regulates our levels of the hormone melatonin. Insufficient bright natural daylight can cause a buildup of melatonin, which can cause depression and lethargy. During long, dark winters, when levels of natural daylight and sun energy are naturally low, this can produce a depressive condition known as seasonal affective disorder, or SAD.

Recent research into so-called "sick building syndrome" has suggested that the air in sealed, air-conditioned office buildings, with windows that do not open, is often very dry. This can make people feel drowsy and less efficient, and may cause headaches, hay fever, and stuffiness. This is because air contains electrically charged particles, called ions, that get charged positively as a result of central heating, air conditioning, cigarette smoke, hot electrical equipment, and overcrowding. A natural environment such as the air on a hilltop or by a waterfall can have around 40,000 negative ions per cubic cm, whereas an air-conditioned office full of computer equipment can have as few as 40.

Furniture, such as a poorly designed desk, mattress, or chair, can encourage bad posture and compound the effects of physical tension. A chair back should be upright, yet relaxed, providing support for the lower lumbar area. You should also be able to place your feet comfortably on the floor in front of you.

The color scheme you choose for a room can induce different moods. Pale blue is a cool color that makes a room more spacious and can often produce feelings of calm and reduce tension, although it can be bleak and cold in a room that receives little sunlight. Yellows, pinks, and oranges are warm, welcoming colors that brighten up a room. Vivid, bright red is the warmest of all the colors; however, research shows that too much red can increase blood pressure, heighten muscle tension, and overstimulate brain activity. Green is a balanced, restful color, and is often used in buildings like hospital wards where people spend a lot of time.

ENVIRONMENT TIPS

- If working indoors, take breaks and get into the natural light as much as possible, or sit close to a window.

- If you work in a dry, sealed centrally heated or air-conditioned office, plants, bowls of water, or an ionizer may help.

- If you cannot escape air-conditioning set the thermostat at 68°F (20°C).

- Minimize the amount of time you are subjected to noise over 85 decibels – a conversation is around 60 db, compared with 100 db for a baby screaming.

- Decorate your home with relaxing furniture and colors that you find conducive to your mental well-being.

PHYSICAL EXERCISE

Keeping fit should be an important part of your stress-control policy. This is especially true if you have a sedentary job. If you are in good physical shape not only are you going to feel happier and more motivated, but you are more likely to be mentally alert.

Regular exercise improves the efficiency of the heart, enhances lung function, maintains good circulation, lowers blood pressure, reduces fat or cholesterol in the blood, and improves the body's immune system. Exercise can protect you from heart disease and help you live longer, and it is also a relaxant, easing muscle tension and reducing symptoms of stress, such as fatigue. During exercise the body releases hormones, such as endorphins, which act as natural anti-depressants and make you feel good. Exercise can improve your self-image and appearance, build your confidence, and increase your energy. It also enables you to distance yourself from the demands of everyday life by distracting you.

A HEALTHY HEART

Regular exercise strengthens the muscles in your body, including your heart muscle. This makes your heart more powerful and efficient so that it can pump a larger quantity of blood with each beat. At rest, a normal heart pumps approximately 1 quart (1 liter) of blood per minute to the muscles, compared with an average of 12 times this volume during exercise. Many of the world's top athletes have a low resting pulse of 40 beats per minute. In contrast, a person who is out of shape, may have a resting pulse rate of 90–100 beats per minute. Another indication

STRETCHING

Before beginning any exercise it is advisable to carry out a few gentle stretching exercises to warm up your muscles and help prevent straining. Start slowly and build up gradually. Do this simple program without any sudden jerks or jolts. Concentrate on keeping the movement fluid. Repeat each exercise for both sides of the body. Wind down for a few minutes afterward.

Arms stretched up as high as you can

Feet flat on floor

1 Start with your arms by your sides, and gently stretch upward.

Arm stretched and bent to left as far as possible

Arm straight down side of body

Feet apart

2 Stretch to one side and hold. This tones the muscles in your side.

Head up and facing forward

Back straight

Hands on hips help keep balance

Leg bent as low as possible

Straight leg

3 Straighten one leg and bend the other as shown to tone inner thigh muscles.

STAMINA, SUPPLENESS, AND STRENGTH

• No real effect   •• Beneficial effect   ••• Very good effect   •••• Excellent effect

EXERCISE	STAMINA	SUPPLENESS	STRENGTH	EXERCISE	STAMINA	SUPPLENESS	STRENGTH
Badminton	••	•••	••	Judo	••	••••	••
Canoeing	•••	••	•••	Rowing	••••	••	••••
Climbing stairs	•••	•	••	Sailing	•	••	••
Cycling (hard)	••••	••	•••	Soccer	•••	•••	•••
Dancing (active)	•••	••••	•	Squash	•••	•••	••
Digging	•••	••	••••	Swimming	••••	••••	••••
Golf	•	••	•	Tennis	••	•••	••
Gymnastics	••	•••	•••	Walking (briskly)	••	•	•
Hill walking	•••	•	••	Weightlifting	•	•	••••
Jogging	••••	••	••	Yoga	•	••••	•

of whether you have a healthy heart is the speed at which your pulse rate returns to normal after vigorous exercise. In a person who exercises regularly the pulse rate returns to resting level within one minute. However, in someone who is not used to getting exercise, it may take as long as five minutes.

Fitness comprises three distinct elements: stamina, suppleness, and strength. Developing all three is the key to well-being and good health. Physical activities that can be performed without a break for at least 12 minutes, such as cycling or jogging, are called aerobic exercise. This is the best type of activity for increasing general levels of fitness, particularly the performance of the heart, lungs, and muscles. Anaerobic exercise, which consists of short, sharp bursts of intense muscle activity, such as squash, is not as helpful for increasing general fitness. Begin your fitness program gently by gradually introducing exercise into your daily routine. Get off the bus one stop earlier and walk the rest of the way, or use the stairs rather than the elevator. You should ideally try to do 20–30 minutes of exercise two or three times a week, slowly building up the intensity. Before you begin, warm up your muscles with gentle stretching. Exercise until you feel tired, not exhausted, and never ignore pain – it is your body's way of saying "stop!" Allow at least one hour after a meal before you start any form of exercise.

Head upright

Stomach muscles held in

Knee in line with ankle

Foot flat on floor

Arms stretched down as far as possible without straining

Legs straight

4 Step back with one foot, keep leg straight, and bend front knee to tone calves.

5 Tone back and leg muscles by touching your toes.

133

HEALTHY EATING

A balanced diet can lift your mood, improve fitness, give you more energy, feed muscles, improve circulation, prevent illness, strengthen your immune system, and make you feel better able to cope with life's stresses. Set regular mealtimes and try to eat three main meals a day, with only light snacks

The key to healthy living is to eat three main meals a day and keep to a varied, balanced diet.

in between. Eating should be a pleasurable and relaxing experience, so always take time to eat, at a table, and enjoy your food.

MORE FIBER AND LESS FAT

Over the years, the guidelines for healthy eating have changed as experts have learned more about the benefits of fiber and the harmful effects of eating too much fat.

The term fiber, or roughage, is the name given to a special group of carbohydrates that includes cereals, beans, peas, vegetables, and fruit. Fiber reduces the amount of cholesterol in your blood and binds the cholesterol in your gut so you do not absorb it. Foods particularly rich in fiber include wholegrain bread, red kidney beans, baked beans, peas, and wholegrain pasta, all of which also contain many other useful vitamins and nutrients. Fiber has the added advantage of not being lost in cooking. It is recommended that adults should eat at least 30 grams of fiber a day.

There are two types of fat. Saturated fats are found in meat, dairy products, solid cooking fat, cookies, chocolates, cakes, and many kinds of chips. Unsaturated fats, or polyunsaturates, are found in sunflower oil, corn oil, and soy oil, nuts, and oily fish, such as herring, mackerel, and trout. A diet that is high in unsaturated fats can cause health problems. First, fat is loaded with calories, which can lead to obesity. Second, too much saturated fat increases the cholesterol level in your blood, clogging your arteries, and putting you at risk of heart disease. Unsaturated fats do not raise cholesterol in the same way, and small amounts are needed by our bodies to help make and repair body cells. Cut down on the total amount of fats you eat, and when you do eat fats, choose ones high in polyunsaturates. An adult's daily intake of fat should not exceed 85 grams.

CUT DOWN ON "MOOD FOODS"

Certain substances, such as salt, sugar, alcohol, and caffeine, can affect your mood. Eaten in excess, these can influence your stress level.
- SALT Everybody needs a daily intake of about 1 gram of salt, yet most of us eat an average of up to 10 grams a day, half of which is added by food manufacturers during processing. For some people, too much salt can lead to high blood pressure, which in turn can lead to strokes and heart disease.
- SUGAR A high intake of sugar gives you a short-term surge of energy. However, as well

> Healthy eating does not mean eating less of everything.

as being fattening and a major cause of tooth decay, in the long term too much sugar can overwork the adrenal glands, depleting the body of strength and causing irritability, lack of concentration, and mood swings.

■ ALCOHOL In the short term, many people feel more relaxed after an alcoholic drink, but too much can reduce your body's ability to withstand stress and cause long-term damage to your health, especially to your liver. Alcoholic drinks also have many calories but few nutrients, and so can lead to obesity.

■ CAFFEINE Coffee, colas, and tea contain caffeine, which is a stimulant that can activate your adrenal glands, increase blood pressure,

stimulate the heart, and mimic the stress response. If you drink too much caffeine your body becomes agitated, and the side effects may well be panic attacks, poor mental control, palpitations, headaches, and migraine.

CONVENIENCE FOOD

Many frozen, canned, and packaged foods are as good as their fresh equivalents. Frozen peas are quick to cook, nutritious, and higher in vitamins than fresh peas, which may have been sitting around for days. Frozen fish is a healthy convenience food, as are canned beans and fruit. Beware of meat products like lunch meat and sausages since they can be high in fat.

TIPS FOR HEALTHY EATING

EAT MORE HIGH-FIBER FOODS
High-fiber foods reduce the risk of heart disease by absorbing the cholesterol in your blood.

FIBER
• Fruit

• Wholegrain bread, flour, and pasta

• Beans, peas, and lentils

• Baked or boiled potatoes with skins on

• Unsalted nuts or dried fruit instead of chips

• Brown rice

EAT MORE LOW-FAT FOODS
Low-fat foods help you stay slim and healthy and keep cholesterol levels down.

• White meat, e.g., chicken
• Skim or low-fat milk

• Raw, boiled, or steamed fresh vegetables served without butter or oily dressing

• Low-fat spread or margarine that is high in polyunsaturates
• Substitute low-fat yogurt for cream
• Grilled, steamed, or baked food
• Fish

AVOID "MOOD FOODS"
Cut out or reduce your intake of the following foods and drinks.

• Tea or coffee – reduce the strength, use decaffeinated or an herbal substitute
• Sugar, in tea and coffee, breakfast cereals, bottled drinks
• Puddings, desserts
• Salt – in cooking and in snacks

EAT LESS FAT
Cut down on all fat, especially saturated fat, which raises cholesterol levels. Always choose polyunsaturated fats.

• Fried foods
• Butter, saturated margarine
• Whole milk
  • Red meat, e.g., beef, lamb
  • Chips, chocolate, cakes
  • Cream, mayonnaise, salad dressing

DEVELOPING HOBBIES AND INTERESTS

Taking up a hobby can be an informal way to meet people and wind down so you are less likely to become stressed.

The conclusion of a recent ten-year study into the causes of happiness was that the best guarantee of long-term happiness is "serious leisure" – a hobby or activity that involves your whole being. It doesn't matter what it is as long as you find it challenging and absorbing. The researchers ranked activities in terms of good feeling or "flow," and dancing ranked top on the list. The explanation for this is that dancing combines the three important ingredients of exercise, music, and social contact. Other high-scoring activities include team sports and involvement with a religious group because of the social contact. Another branch of research has shown that caring for a pet gives happiness, makes you feel wanted, and brings additional meaning to life. Simply stroking a pet or watching a fish swim in an aquarium can reduce heartbeat, blood pressure, and levels of stress.

Developing new interests involves taking risks or being prepared to explore the unknown and break away from your familiar "comfort zone." If you join a new club or take a course, you should expect to feel frustrated initially, since you will have to get to know new people and may feel that you are not involved or do not fit in. Satisfaction and pleasure may not be instantaneous, and you must be ready to persevere until the situation improves. Be confident, and do not worry about what other people might think. For example, if you started singing in a choir, you might find yourself thinking, "They might not like my voice" or "People will think I should be at home with the children on a Saturday morning, not enjoying myself in a choir." Challenge these negative irrational thoughts (*see pp.106–107*). Developing new interests requires a positive approach. Even if things do not work out, you need to be able to tell yourself, "It's not a failure because I've learned something."

Research has shown that if we have no hobbies or interests to absorb and challenge us, we tend to get stressed, depressed, discouraged, and bored. If we are not careful, a vicious circle can develop in which the less we do, the more miserable we feel, and as we become more unhappy we are less willing to take risks and try new activities.

PLAN YOUR LEISURE TIME

This simple exercise will help you decide how you want to spend your free time

- List 20 activities that you have enjoyed over the past ten years. For example, going to the seashore, having friends over for dinner, walking in the country.

- List 10 activities that you do not do, but that you would like to pursue.

- Make yourself a promise now to do one activity from each list in the next month. Write down what you will have to do to fit in these two new activities.

EXPANDING YOUR CIRCLE OF FRIENDS

Research indicates that an extensive social network is one of the most important insulators against stress. One study has shown that women who had one important confiding relationship were 90 percent less likely to become depressed than women who had no such relationship. Social contact offers us the option to express our feelings, providing us with feedback and sometimes useful information and practical help. Some people are good at making friends, most of us have to work at it. One recent study showed that 80 percent of people said that at some point in their lives they were shy, in the sense of being anxious about meeting people and suffering discomfort in the presence of others.

The challenge is to make social contact with people we pass in everyday life and to develop these contacts into friendships. There are many theories as to the best way to do this, but the simplest way is to develop a genuine interest in the other person. When you meet, smile and address him or her by name. Try to make the person feel important. Encourage conversation, and listen attentively.

The first hurdle is to overcome your fear of rejection. Accept that rejection is part of everyday life and seek it out. Say to yourself, "I'm going to start a conversation with eight people this week even if I am rejected by half of them." If you think people might find you boring, learn to replace these negative self-statements with positive statements: for example, "Most other people worry about being boring. I do have interesting things to say." Find your own statements that defeat this negative self-talk. Worry less about what people will think of you, and think more about being yourself.

> Confiding in a friend helps reduce stress levels.

WIDEN YOUR SOCIAL CIRCLE

1 BE FRIENDLY
Show people around you that you are friendly. Say "Good morning" to the mail carrier, paper boy, or store clerk.

2 TALK TO PEOPLE
Spend five minutes engaged in small talk with a neighbor. Join in a coffee break at work, or take part in a social gathering.

3 JOIN IN
Enroll in a course, or join an evening course or a club. Take the plunge – it will get easier with time.

4 MAKE CONTACT
Call or write to an old friend or somebody you like but with whom you have lost contact.

5 SEND CARDS
Write and send Christmas cards, vacation postcards, birthday cards, and letters.

6 MAKE AN EFFORT
List people you would like to know better. Make an effort to talk to them. When appropriate, invite them for a drink or meal.

TWELVE STEPS TO POSITIVE MENTAL HEALTH

Psychology has come a long way since the days of Sigmund Freud digging into the secrets of people's past lives. We now understand much more about how we create our own emotional distress. The ingredients for stress and poor mental health are a combination of demanding life events and inadequate life skills. Most people who have extreme stress or emotional problems do not have a medical condition, they are not sick. Rather, they have acquired self-defeating behavior patterns or poor coping skills. Just as we have learned to think and act in a way that causes us to be stressed, we can learn to change those behaviors and thinking patterns and acquire new skills. These ideas are the cornerstones to the "self-help" movement. In many situations we might not require in-depth therapy, but we need to be taught these essential life skills. Without doubt, we feel unhappy when experiencing prolonged stress. If we can discover ways of managing that stress, does it not follow that we will feel happier?

A reasonable definition of happiness might be Dr. John Schindler's when he said, "Happiness is a state of mind in which our thinking is pleasant a good share of the time." What makes you happy? People often assume that more money, a new car, more friends, a new relationship, family, success, status, material belongings, or a variety of other things can make you happy. None of these things makes you happy in isolation. You make yourself happy by the way you think and act.

Certain ways of thinking and acting are likely to lead to fulfillment and positive mental health, just as the opposite ways of thinking and behaving are predisposers to stress and unhappiness.

The following steps summarize most of the life skills covered in this book. Most stressed people are likely to have weakness in some of these skills. To maintain all 12 steps is, of course, an ideal we all work toward. Bear in mind that you will need to have accomplished the earlier steps before moving on to the later ones.

1 TAKE RESPONSIBILITY FOR YOUR OWN LIFE

You are responsible for your thoughts, actions, feelings, decisions, and their consequences. Unless you take responsibility you will not strive to change what can be changed. Rather, you will blame other people or life events for the way you think and feel. A person who does not take responsibility is a victim.

2 BE FLEXIBLE IN YOUR THINKING

We all have needs, but when these become too demanding we become stressed. Try to adopt a flexible philosophy – change what you can change and adjust to what you can't change. Eliminate absolutist thinking, such as "should," "ought to," and "must," from your vocabulary.

3 ACCEPT REALITY AS A MIXTURE OF GOOD AND BAD

Accept the reality of unfairness, accept that you are not always right, accept that things change, and accept that circumstances are not usually clear-cut or black and white. The world, just like you, is a mixture of good and bad rather than all bad or all good. Accept that it is okay to be "good enough."

6 ACCEPT AND TAKE CARE OF YOURSELF

We are all fallible, complex mixtures of good and bad, strengths and weaknesses. Accept that you are unique. Like yourself, or at least find parts of yourself that you like. Be committed to taking care of yourself, challenging any "guilt" that this might engender. Take care of your body, eat healthy food, and exercise. Treat yourself with rewards.

9 THINK RATIONALLY AND CREATIVELY

Formulate your own solutions, rather than accepting what you have been told. What alternative views are there? Reevaluate messages from your childhood. Identify and challenge absolutist, rigid thinking and beware of thinking distortions. Put yourself in control of the decisions you make in your life. At the same time, encourage creativity and spontaneity.

12 DEVELOP AND MAINTAIN RELATIONSHIPS

Value and nurture friendships and show commitment. Communicate openly, and be a good listener. Accept others for what they are, rather than trying to change them. Try not to be critical. Develop a network of support. Make a standing date with your spouse, confidant, best friend, or children. Value people with whom you feel relaxed and can be yourself.

5 LEARN TO LIVE WITH FRUSTRATION

Build your tolerance of frustration by putting yourself into frustrating situations. View the situation as a challenge rather than something to avoid. Challenge your underlying beliefs that *"I can't stand it"* with *"I don't like it, but I can stand it."* Frustration is a necessary part of life and important for any personal progress.

8 WORK TOWARD GOALS

Identify and own what you want out of life and what is important to you. Make sure that your goals are both short- and long-term in all areas of your life. These goals give your life direction and meaning. Be committed but not rigid. Make sure that these goals are not contradictory nor too demanding. Accept that there will be short-term frustrations in working toward any long-term goal.

11 DEVELOP HOBBIES AND ABSORBING INTERESTS

Experiment until you find an interest that is absorbing, meaningful, and fulfilling to you and then pursue it. Commit yourself to your new interest and invest time and energy. If this activity is work, develop other interests to counterbalance it. Aim for a variety of interests in case one fails.

4 SAVOR THE MOMENT

At times slow down and reflect on the world around you and what is important in your life. Set goals that give you direction, but do not be a slave to them. Enjoy the journey to the goal, rather than just arriving at a destination. Deliberately vary the pace of your life, mixing periods of activity with periods of calm. Seek out laughter, fun, change, and creativity.

7 EXPRESS POSITIVE AND NEGATIVE FEELINGS

Express your thoughts, feelings, and emotions in an open, assertive way without violating the rights of others. Learn to say no. Accept that others may have different preferences and that this may result in anger, sadness, and disappointment, which need to be expressed. Seek out and communicate laughter.

10 MANAGE YOUR TIME AND MAINTAIN A BALANCE

Achieve a balance between work and leisure, family and friends, being serious and having fun, and being with people and being alone. Know what you want out of life and set your own agenda and priorities. Occasionally set aside time to contemplate what are the important values in life and whether you are maintaining a balance.

INDEX

T

talking, 116–17
tantrums, 53
tea, 35, 135
temper tantrums, 53
temporalis muscles, 38
tension, 38, 128
thinking, *see* thoughts
thoracic breathing, 130
thoughts
  chronic fatigue, 36
  and depression, 25
  distorted thinking, 105–8
  ladder your thoughts, 110
  obsessive behavior, 21
  rational thinking, 104–13
  rigid thinking, 109
  stopping unwanted
    thoughts, 21
time management, 94–103

delegation, 100–1
goal planning, 96–7
hurry sickness, 102–3
perfectionism, 99
procrastination, 98
tiredness, 36
tranquilizer addiction, 33
trauma, 66–7
triggers
  anger, 26, 27
  depression, 24
  headaches, 38–9
Type A behavior, 102–3
Type B behavior, 102–3
"tyranny of the shoulds," 109

U V W

unemployment, 76–7
universal "should," 109
uselessness, sense of, 29

values, shared, 49
visualization
  goal planning, 97
  living with pain, 57
  and self-esteem, 37
weddings, 48
weight
  eating disorders, 28–9
  high blood pressure, 40
wind, 41
withdrawal
  smoking, 32
  tranquilizers, 33
work
  coping with work stress, 75
  delegation, 100–1
  environmental stress, 131
  life without work, 76–7
  midlife crisis, 63
  stress questionnaire, 74–5
worries, demolishing, 112–13

ACKNOWLEDGMENTS

PAGE*One* would like to take this opportunity to thank the following people for their help in making this book: Steve Gorton for photography; Anthony Duke for the illustrations; Dr. G. T. Parker for checking the text for medical accuracy; Hilary Bird for compiling the index; Lorri Baker and Barry O'Rourke from Galloways Two, Parese Jackson and Ben Myhill from GP Associates, and Angela Jackson, Aszerina Robinson, and Sarah Watson for modeling; Karen Gibilaro from Artistic Licence for doing the makeup; Chris Clark for DTP design; Matthew Cook for design assistance.

THE AUTHOR would like to thank his wife, Meriel Powell, for reading and commenting on the text and for being a source of inspiration.

PICTURE CREDITS
Many thanks to the picture libraries and photographers for their kind permission to reproduce the following photographs in this book:

2 Robert Harding Picture Library/Schuster; 6 Paul Bricknell; 9 DIAF/Philippe Cannic; 14–15 Tony Stone Images/Lori Adamski Peek; 42–43 The Image Bank/Larry Dale Gordon; 78–79 Tony Stone Images/Dan Bosler; 82 Tony Stone Images/Dan Bosler; 88 Tony Stone Images/ Bruce Ayers; 89 The Image Bank/Al Hamdan; 94 Tony Stone Images/David Madison; 104 Tony Stone Images/David Young Wolff; 114 Tony Stone Images/Dan Bosler; 134 Arnald Mackechnie; 135 Colin Walton; 136 Camera Press/Lars Matzen.

PICTURE RESEARCHER
Nadine Bazar

NOTE
The questionnaire on pp.44–45 is loosely based on Holmes and Rahe (1967) "The Social Readjustment Rating Scale," Journal of Psychomatic Research, 1967, II, 213–218.